ELITES, MASSES, AND MODERNIZATION IN LATIN AMERICA,
1850–1930

*The Texas Pan American Series*

# Elites, Masses, and Modernization in Latin America, 1850–1930

By E. Bradford Burns and Thomas E. Skidmore
Introduction by Richard Graham
Edited by Virginia Bernhard

University of Texas Press, Austin and London

*The Texas Pan American Series is published with the assistance of a revolving publication fund established by the Pan American Sulphur Company.*

4114

**Library of Congress Cataloging in Publication Data**
Main entry under title:

Elites, masses, and modernization in Latin America, 1850–1930.

   Two lectures originally presented at the University of St. Thomas in Houston in 1978, rev. for publication.
   Includes bibliographical references.
   CONTENTS: Graham, R. Popular challenges and elite responses: an introduction.—Burns, E. B. Cultures in conflict: the implication of modernization in nineteenth-century Latin America.—Skidmore, T. E. Workers and soldiers: urban labor movements and elite responses in twentieth-century Latin America.
   1. Latin America—Social conditions—Addresses, essays, lectures.
   2. Latin America—Economic conditions—Addresses, essays, lectures.
   3. Elite (Social sciences)—Latin America—Addresses, essays, lectures.
   4. Culture conflict—Latin America—Addresses, essays, lectures.
   5. Industrial relations—Latin America—Addresses, essays, lectures.
I. Burns, E. Bradford. Cultures in conflict. 1979.   II. Skidmore, Thomas E. Workers and soldiers. 1979.   III. Bernhard, Virginia, 1937–
HN110.5.A8E54     309.1'8'003     79-14785
ISBN 0-292-76457-X

*Requests for permission to reproduce material in this work should be sent to: Permissions, University of Texas Press, Box 7819, Austin, Texas 78712.*

# Contents

# Foreword

IN 1957 THE FAMILY and friends of the late Benjamin Kopper Smith established the B. K. Smith Chair in History at the University of St. Thomas in Houston, Texas, in memory of a former German bellmaker who had an avid interest in the history of his adopted country.

Smith's own history is an American success story. Born in Dresden, Germany, in 1882, he came to the United States as a young man and found work as a welder in a railroad shop. He soon rose to be welding superintendent on the Pennsylvania Railroad. In 1920 he and an associate came to Texas and founded the Big Three Welding and Equipment Company. It was an eminently successful venture, and Smith's contributions to the Houston community were noteworthy.

The B. K. Smith Chair in History is a fitting memorial to this man. It has enabled the History Department periodically to invite distinguished historians to the campus. In addition to visiting classes and holding informal discussions with students and faculty, each visiting historian delivers a special lecture for the general public and the academic community. In 1978 the History Department invited two scholars in the field of Latin American history, Dr. E. Bradford Burns and Dr. Thomas E. Skidmore, to choose a subject of common interest and to present lectures from contrasting viewpoints. Their lectures were presented under the title "Popular Challenges and Elite Responses in Latin America, 1850–1930," and have been revised for publication in this volume.

E. Bradford Burns is Professor of History at the University of California at Los Angeles. He is the author of a prize-winning study entitled *The Unwritten Alliance: Rio Branco and Brazilian-American Relations* (1966). His most recent work is the revised edition of *Latin America: A Concise Interpretive History* (1972, 1977). Dr. Burns holds the Order of Rio Branco, conferred by the government of Brazil.

Thomas E. Skidmore, Professor of History at the University of Wisconsin, is the author of *Black into White: Race and Nationality in Brazilian Thought* (1974). An earlier book, *Politics in Brazil, 1930–1964: An Experiment in Democracy* (1967), has been reprinted several times in both English and Portuguese editions. Dr. Skidmore is a past president of the Latin American Studies Association.

Richard Graham, Professor of History at the University of Texas at Austin and himself a distinguished Latin Americanist, served as commentator and has written the Introduction to the volume. His most recent books are *Independence in Latin America: A Comparative Approach* (1972) and *Britain and the Onset of Modernization in Brazil, 1850–1914* (1968, 1972).

Virginia Bernhard, the editor of this volume, is Professor of History at the University of St. Thomas.

Ann Q. Tiller
*Chairman, History Department*
*University of St. Thomas*

ELITES, MASSES, AND MODERNIZATION IN LATIN AMERICA,
1850–1930

*Richard Graham*   **Popular Challenges and Elite Responses: An Introduction**

THE PAST informs the present. As Latin Americans and North Americans mutually explore their histories, they gain a clearer vision of their current differences and similarities. In the present volume two eminent North American historians discuss hitherto neglected facets of the Latin American past and, in doing so, almost inadvertently highlight—by the evident contrast with the North American past—aspects of the United States's formation that have not been sufficiently examined. Using these essays we can make comparisons with the North American experience and thus learn more about the history of the United States.

There was a time when history consisted of the deeds of famous men. But in these essays historians relate what ordinary people did and thought and how they struggled against their "betters." The stance of the elites and the masses toward each other in Latin America today derives from these past experiences and will doubtless influence the course of their future connection. Our understanding of Latin America is thus significantly deepened by our attention to these essays.

The University of St. Thomas is especially to be commended for making these papers available to a wider audience outside the confines of academia. Historians too often write for each other, but the issues dealt with are too important to be left to them alone.

E. Bradford Burns here sketches in broad strokes the cultural history of all Latin America in the nineteenth century, revealing a penetrating knowledge of an enormous literature. He marshals his erudition to advance the view that two cultures were in conflict: that of the modernizing, European-oriented elite and that of the "common folk" of mixed racial background who lived close to the earth. In addition, he raises the existential questions posed by the alleged progress of science and industry.

Thomas E. Skidmore points to the emerging field of labor history in twentieth-century Latin America and suggests the historical roots of today's exacerbated tensions in that area. The torture, terror, and violence practiced by military leaders today are put in the context of a secular struggle of army against workers. At the same time he specifies how union leaders have been systematically co-opted and disciplined to serve as tools of the dominant classes.

There are several similarities in the two approaches. Both authors are concerned to note the failures of earlier historians to understand fully the complexities of the problems they encountered. Skidmore notes the recent rise of interest both in Latin America and in the United States in the study of labor history in contrast to an earlier fascination with only the elite. Burns suggests, at times more implicitly than explicitly, that historians have been too prone to present a "Whig" interpretation, that is, too ready to concentrate on the innovative victors and too reluctant to note the force and significance of those who opposed change. Historians in Latin America, Burns says, have been too ready to project a vision of the past born of their own upper-class position. Like Skidmore, he asks us to focus on the non-elite, the ordinary people of Latin America.

Both writers are critical of the liberal developmentalism that characterized North American thinking about Latin America in the 1960s. That was a period when social scientists in general, along with policy makers, believed in the possibility of steady and gradual change toward a polity modeled on that of the United States and built on principles of individual liberties derived from John Locke. Development came to be understood as part of a series of social, economic, and intellectual changes often summed up by the word *modernization*. In contrast, Latin American historians and social scientists were wary. They saw modernization as Burns does here as only a "cosmetic" that did not include profound alterations of those inherited structures that benefited the elite.

Skidmore points out that, as the 1960s wore on, North American academics, like their Latin American colleagues, lost their blind faith in incremental change without rupture or conflict. They may have been brought to this realization more quickly because they saw the ugly underbelly of North American interventionism in Latin America and elsewhere: if mild reform would not work, U.S. policy makers preferred to support brutal repression than to tolerate radical change. Historians too long lent their voice of support—by the conceptual tools they used—to the scramble toward modernization without sufficient concern for the deep structural shifts and accompanying social upheaval necessary to effect genuine change. As Skidmore acknowledges, any real alteration in the conditions of labor required reversals in the power relations of society as a whole. Social scientists of the past decade reflected, albeit unconsciously, the desires of an American ruling class for a kind of change in the Third World that would increase opportunities for this class without threatening an established order. Whether our present heightened awareness of what was going on in the 1960s can alter this push toward the globalization of capitalist enterprise in any significant way is probably in doubt; social scientists are not as influential when they criticize the structure of society as when they defend it.

To extract the greatest profit from the essays in this volume, the reader may wish to keep some questions in mind. Burns, choosing to shun an approach that would highlight Latin American class divisions, does not discuss what economic interests were served by those nineteenth-century elites who either turned to foreign-inspired progress for salvation or opted for the maintenance of traditional values. The reader may profitably ask this question and seek the answer in the evidence Burns presents. Skidmore has focused his attention on the apparent hate the military directed at the laborers, without considering whose interests that animosity served. The army itself does not gain much direct advantage from such an attitude. What class or classes benefit from the sol-

diers' stance? Similarly, if the United States government has
supported military coups, have all Americans or only certain
ones profited thereby?

Both authors tend to see society as made up of two groups:
elite and mass. Does this dichotomy cloud particular economic interests? Elites differ from nation to nation and from sector
to sector and may even be divided within themselves, but the
concept of elites tends to blur the distinctions. Just as modernization has been discussed elsewhere[1] as if all such pro-
cesses were the same, all modernizers alike, and all modern
societies basically identifiable with each other, without considering the radical differences among them in terms of class
dominance, Skidmore and Burns in these works tend to ignore the different interests served by various elites. Cuban
and Brazilian elites today, for instance, tend in such radically
divergent directions that the use of one term for both shows
the frailty of the very notion of elites.

A related question is one of categories. How does Burns
decide who was a member of the "folk" and who was not? Is
it because they behaved a certain way? If he were to extend
the time-frame of his paper into the period covered by Skidmore, would Burns discard from the folk those workers who
applauded the spread of factory employment? In short, is the
folk—like the elite—too vague a category?

Both Burns and Skidmore stress the role of ideas. Skidmore argues, along with most other labor historians, that the
working class in early twentieth-century Latin America was
much influenced by anarchist ideas imported from Europe.
But it is worth considering whether or not these ideas were
chosen because they fit a particular situation in Latin America. Similarly, Latin America's fascist solutions of the 1930s
and later—although on the surface copied from Europe—may
represent choices made by individuals who found them con-
sonant with the needs of their social class. Similar preferences
appeared in the nineteenth century, and the reader may wish,
when reading Burns's essay, to keep constantly in mind who
made these choices. Ideas do not have a life of their own,
choosing where to go or whom to influence; it is real women
and men who think and act. On the other hand, ideas *are*

important, and, while reading these essays, the reader may keep in mind that ideas work in mutual relationship to society or to economy: sometimes they mesh, sometimes they jar.

Burns is to be congratulated for writing about culture when for so long it has been structure that has drawn the attention of historians. Meanings and understandings are as central to the historian as to the anthropologist, and such a focus is long overdue. Burns's treatment of culture nevertheless raises some particular questions. Is it fair to define culture as a set of ideas for the elite but as a set of beliefs and attitudes for the common folk? Is there not an equally unspecified and unwritten code operating for the members of the elite in their daily life? If we examine not their books and speeches but their mode of interrelating with others, even the modernizers may be found to be living according to the norms of a traditional society. City dwellers may also live in community and not necessarily suffer anomie.

Burns sees the elite from the "inside," so to speak, taking their statements at face value, examining what they said. But he looks at the common folk from the "outside," and judges their thoughts on the basis of what they did, not what they said. Skidmore similarly examines only what labor leaders said, while he sees the workers as a group to be controlled and manipulated. The reader may ask what ordinary workers thought was being accomplished. How did they view the employers? What did they think of the State? Did they want a different kind of labor organization? Sources with which to answer such questions are not as hard to find as both authors seem to think.[2] Social scientists are increasingly finding ways of making so-called inarticulate groups speak, and, as scholars continue to examine the culture of folk and workers, they will probably find more change over time than is evident in these papers.

The reader may also ask whether we should not discard the conceptual scheme of modernization altogether, instead of doing as Burns suggests and merely turning our gaze on the opponents of modernization. Like Ferdinand Tönnies almost a century ago, Burns expresses a nostalgia for *gemeinschaft*, for corporate community rather than atomistic society, for—

in Burns's words—the "well-defined moral order in which each person knew his role and the interrelationships of individuals."[3] As may many of Burns's readers, I share his skepticism about "progress," especially since in Latin America it has so often meant that the lot of the common people has worsened. But this kind of progress is not the only alternative to a traditional, nearly medieval society.

Furthermore, in the "unity" and "harmony" sought by the nineteenth-century folk and in the social world Burns portrays in which there was a "mutual devotion of leader and masses,"[4] the reader may see even more ominous signs. It is not surprising that the biographer of one of these leaders was Manuel Gálvez, the Argentine protofascist. To be sure, in nineteenth-century Latin America there were efforts to maintain a traditional society. Burns does us a service by bringing together accounts of these efforts, whose origins lie deep in the history of colonial Latin America. But before readers give as much approbation to these conservative forces as does Burns, they should ask where such conservatism led. Was it not precisely to the corporatist approaches of those twentieth-century leaders described in Skidmore's essay? In Chile military officers in the 1920s worked to bring about harmony between capital and labor through a labor code that discouraged "competitive unionization" and "subjected unions to very close supervision by the government."[5] Juan Perón in Argentina in the 1940s and 1950s and Getúlio Vargas in Brazil a decade earlier constructed similar systems, not for individuals acting cooperatively to shape the direction of their lives, but for corporate bodies, of workers or employers or churchmen, for example, directed from the top down. One such corporate body—the army—had since colonial times jealously guarded its special rights and privileges like those of a medieval estate. And it is this corporate tradition that is still invoked when soldiers now turn against workers.

So today we face the heritage of that heroic nineteenth-century struggle described by Burns: it prevented the spread of those forensic categories of thought characteristic of the North Atlantic world. The undefined "people" and "folk" of Burns's nineteenth century are now the "working class" described by Skidmore, and they reap the bitter harvest of their ancestors' struggle against modernity.

The richly provocative essays that follow raise issues central to our times. The United States avoided the corporatist state described by Skidmore and foreshadowed by the groups studied by Burns. Is this not because the English-speaking world underwent a social revolution that culminated in the bloody civil wars of the seventeenth century (often called the Puritan Revolution)? But in Latin America a society of estates did not violently give way to a society of classes. Those Latin American elites to which both authors refer did not spring from any such dislocating movement and did not, therefore, newly construct a set of beliefs and attitudes in keeping with the struggle of a bourgeoisie to capture power. In the nineteenth century these elites appealed to a vision of progress drawn from the North Atlantic world without accepting the social implications of that vision. As Burns notes, they did not undertake—nor could they have been expected to undertake—revisions in the land-tenure system. Even their notion of the State was more in keeping with that of Auguste Comte—whose influence in his native France was minimal—than with the democratic principles that were increasingly put into practice in those very countries these elites sought to emulate. Simultaneously, some members of the elite even shunned modernization, preferring the political and religious traditions earlier imported from the Iberian peninsula or molded out of an American past. In none of these cases were structural alterations in society fully considered (although the complaint voiced by the people that, for the rich "there is no law, no judge, no prison"[6] suggests that some were not unaware of the problem). In short, Latin America had no social revolution.

The capitalist industrialization that has taken place there sprang from very different impulses and could not fail to project very different results. By erecting high tariffs, Latin American governments have deliberately encouraged multinational corporations to invest within their territories, build factories, and thus substitute locally made products for goods previously imported. Such a process required little structural change and merely consolidated the client economies and polities of Latin America. The major beneficiaries of the process have been the collaborating elites within Latin America and North American business interests; little wealth or power has accrued to newly risen groups and virtually none to urban workers or peasants. The elite response to popular challenges has, on the whole, been firm and uncompromising.

But today the power of those dominant elites may be waning. Evidence for this is the very intensification of their repressive action. In the face of increasing threats to their position, they seem demoralized and appear to lack *savoir faire*. No longer is there unquestioned acceptance of capitalist models of development among the elites themselves. Intellectuals who once seconded the importation of these models now increasingly abandon that sinking ship. The best evidence of all is the very violence, sometimes brutal, sometimes subtle, that elites now require to hold workers in line. And violence on one side stores up violence on the other.

Where will the U.S. stand in such an eventuality? Is it not time for its revolutionary heritage to reawaken? Skidmore and Burns, by raising broad interpretive questions about the Latin American past in these essays, stimulate our thinking about the future—not only that of Latin America but that of North America as well.

*E. Bradford Burns* **Cultures in Conflict: The Implication of Modernization in Nineteenth-Century Latin America**

CULTURAL CONFLICT characterized nineteenth-century Latin America. On the one hand, the elites, increasingly enamored with the modernization first of an industrializing Europe and then of the United States, insisted on importing those foreign patterns and imposing them on their own fledgling nations. On the other hand, the vast majority of Latin Americans, including some elites but most particularly the popular classes, recognized the threat inherent in the wholesale importation of modernization and the capitalism accompanying it. They resisted modernization, preferring their long-established living patterns to the more recent foreign novelties and fearing the impact of capitalism on their lives. The conflict between these groups intensified as the century matured because the elites became increasingly convinced that Europe and the United States offered solutions to the problems they perceived in their societies as well as a life-style to their liking. In the ensuing struggle the Europeanized elites did not hesitate to repress violently the opposing majority which clung to its preferences and, when necessary, used physical means in an effort to preserve them.

North Atlantic capitalism engulfed Latin America in the nineteenth century as the elites encouraged modernization. True, in many parts of Latin America, by the opening of the century a type of neo-capitalism already had penetrated and, under Iberian institutions, had long since influenced Indian society. This neo-capitalism continued to shape at least a part of local customs as they evolved over the centuries. However, to a greater or lesser degree, depending on the area, the Iberian authorities had worked out with the inhabitants of their New World empires a *modus operandi* which respected or tolerated many local customs. If the local populations converted nominally to Roman Catholicism, acknowledged the supremacy of Iberian monarchs, and supplied labor when needed by the Europeans, they were largely left alone. Also, they received a kind of protection from Crown and Church as well as a certain minimal security from the local neo-feudalistic landowners. In short, a type of compromise had been reached between Iberian demands and local customs. Like most compromises it suited neither side perfectly, but both accepted it as preferable to other alternatives. At any rate, the penetration of that Iberian neo-capitalism was incomplete and was by no means as challenging to the local populations after the initial conquest period as was North Atlantic capitalism after 1821, particularly after mid-century.

Profoundly altering the concepts of land and labor, North Atlantic capitalism clashed with the practices and ideology of the Latin American folk. The lands the folk once used, often lands which served entire communities and constituted a fundamental factor in personal, environmental, and ecological relationships, became a commodity to be bought and sold. Lands which had succeeded in remaining outside of or peripheral to Iberian neo-capitalism passed from community control into the hands of fewer and fewer owners. These owners often withheld the lands from use, either as an investment or as one means of dominating a scarce labor supply, or cultivated them to produce items which had little or no local use but sold profitably in distant markets. By the end of the century, the folk had lost control of most of the lands they once had worked. Further, they were forced to sell their labor for a minimal return to the hacienda and plantation owners and, under that arrangement, some of them were employed only a few months of each year. At the same time that land was concentrated in fewer hands, the population rose rapidly, jumping from approximately 30.5 million in 1850 to 61 million by 1900. The problems caused by an expanding population and restricted landowning can be readily understood.

Since the labor of these folk and their relationship to the land had constituted well-established patterns of behavior, the rapid and extensive change to commercial agriculture and to an export economy traumatized their lives. Relentlessly challenged by the export sector, the folk societies disintegrated. Each phase of modernization seemed to increase the pressure. Local communities became a part of a larger, more distant, more impersonal, and more pervasive economic system to which the folk sacrificed their land, labor, and life-styles but from which they received scant benefits or none at all. Those changes, to meet the rising demands of distant metropolises, transcended the realm of economics and challenged long-established cultural values.

The selection of cultural conflict as a major means of viewing the nineteenth century provides a useful guide for the interpretation of Latin American history, but, like all general theories which sweep across vast geographic and temporal spaces, it contains weaknesses as well as strengths. For one thing, we know far more about elite preferences than popular ones, and hence we tend to see the elitist view of the past with greater precision and will continue to do so until more research better clarifies the alternatives. For another, it is difficult to generalize about the diverse peoples and myriad events which compose a century of the history of such a varied area as Latin America. Nonetheless, the thesis of cultural conflict would seem to contain sufficient validity to provide a useful insight into and better understanding of a period of the Latin American past which is confusing and seldom handled interpretively. Further, this interpretation of the first century of Latin American independence helps to explain some of the major problems of contemporary Latin America, in particular those revolving around questions of development.

The first temptation raised by this interpretation is to see the cultural conflict in terms of class struggle, which doubtless was present. But that oversimplification should be avoided in view of the richness and complexity of the myriad events of nineteenth-century Latin America. True, generally speaking, those favoring the shaping of Latin America in the

European–United States image with the attendant modernization and imposition of capitalism were associated with the
upper classes, the socioeconomic and political elites. After all,
they enjoyed the readiest access to North Atlantic ideas and
seemed best situated to benefit from modernization. It is
equally true, however, that large numbers of the elites hesi-
tated to embrace the ideas and ways of Northern Europe and
the United States, clinging to the Iberian past and the American experience. The interests of the traditional rural patriarchs did not always harmonize with those of the merchants,
bureaucrats, and other members of the increasingly affluent
urban bourgeoisie. Whereas the economic inclinations of both
groups might have dictated continued if not intensified exportation of agrarian and mineral products, the cultural preferences of the patriarchs and the bourgeoisie separated them.
The former maintained a greater loyalty to the past, while the
latter sighed for a Europeanized future. Although the masses
swayed often to favor various positions, most of them evinced
a loyalty to life-styles associated with folk cultures, a term
and concept on which this essay expands later. The flexibility
of the masses and more particularly of the elites confounds
the class-struggle approach. Yet a struggle there was, and if
not along clearly delineated class lines, then surely among
cultural preferences.

In its attempt to provide an interpretative thesis for nineteenth-century Latin American history, this essay will focus
first on the faith exalted by members of the elites in Europeanization and the modernization—or, to use the word they so
often employed in the nineteenth century, "progress"—which
in their eyes accompanied it. Second, this study will consider
the reservations and the alternatives of other members of the
same elites, before moving to the more difficult problem of
determining the desires of the greater numbers of the humbler
classes, by far the majority, in Latin America. In most cases
rapid modernization threatened the more static folk societies,
and as the thrust to modernize intensified, a clash between its
advocates and the folk became inevitable. Violence emerged
as a leitmotif of the nineteenth century.

## The Elite Preference

The Latin American elites of the nineteenth century boasted of their European heritage, and even those with Indian and/or African ancestors dwelt more on their European ties. They understood what was happening in Europe and easily discussed the latest ideas radiating from the Old World, which they welcomed to the New. Generally speaking, three major European philosophies shaped their ideas during the nineteenth century: the Enlightenment, the ideas of evolution put forth by Charles Darwin and Herbert Spencer, and Positivism. Interconnected, the three found a common nexus in the concept of "progress," the key word for the understanding of nineteenth-century Latin American history.

Teaching the vincibility of ignorance, the Enlightenment philosophers concluded that if people had the opportunity to know the truth, they would select "civilization" over "barbarism." Adherents to the Enlightenment believed in a universally valid standard to judge "civilization," and the criteria for such a judgment were based on European concepts of progress. Civilization and the progress which led to it became identified with Europe, or more specifically with England, France, and Germany. However, a burgeoning faith in science directed judgments on progress as well as progress itself away from philosophical and moral matters toward material change. The popularized idea of Darwin, that organic forms developed over the course of time and represented successive stages in a single evolutionary process, further heightened the interest in progress, giving it in fact a scientific veneer. Very propitiously, Spencer, who enjoyed tremendous circulation in nineteenth-century Latin America, applied the same principle of evolution to society. Progress to Spencer signified a march toward "the establishment of the greatest perfection and the most complete happiness." However, that march subsumed a great many economic changes and adaptations. As one example, Spencer advocated railroads as a vital part of the organic system of a modern society. As another, he regarded industrialization as a certain manifestation of progress. The Latin

Americans drew from Spencer the idea of the interrelation-
ship of science, industry, and progress, a combination point-
ing to future glory through societal evolution. Like most European thinkers, Spencer had much to say—racist statements,
for example—which damned Latin America. The Latin Americans proved to be selective readers, however, and chose to
ignore what displeased—or frightened—them.

Many of the ideas on progress drawn from the Enlightenment, Darwin, Spencer, and other sources seemed to come
together in the form Auguste Comte's Positivism assumed in
Latin America during the last decades of the century. Positivism affirmed that social evolution and progress were inevitable. To Comte, that progress was attainable through the
acceptance of scientific laws codified by Positivism. Outward
manifestations of progress—again, railroads and industrialization—assumed great importance in Positivism and emphati-
cally so among the Latin Americans, whether they acknowledged Comte or not.

Clearly those intellectual mentors satisfied the longings
of part of the Latin American elites to replicate European
"civilization" in their hemisphere, which to their thinking
evinced all too many "barbaric" Indian and African traits.
Over the course of the century, the elites distilled a philosophical overview which approved European "progress" in Latin
American terms. Politically, they required order to imple-
ment it. Economically, they adopted capitalism, which
seemed to have transformed England into a modern nation,
to finance it. Further, as the century matured, many Latin
Americans thought they witnessed in the experience of the
United States a verification of the results of implementing
European ideas in the New World. After all, the United States
once had been a colony too, and yet by mid-century it seemed
well on the way to modernizing. Certainly progress seemed
obvious in the post–Civil War period, which boasted of the
continental expansion of the railroads and the triumph of industrialization. The elite attributed the success of the United
States to two factors: the preponderance of Europeans in the
racial composition and the adoption of European ideology,
political as well as economic. In short, the United States rep-

resented in their eyes the success of Europeanization in the New World.[1] Europeanization (or any of the synonyms or euphemisms: Westernization, modernization, or progress) meant to them, as the experience of the U.S. emphasized, the implementation of patterns from France, England, and Germany, since they ignored or deprecated Iberian and Mediterranean Europe as "backward."

Some of the elites had initiated a serious and escalating questioning of some of the Iberian values during the last decades of the eighteenth century. It goes without saying that they were even more critical of Indian and African contributions to Latin American life, if, in fact, they ever considered them. Increased contacts with Northern Europeans, an expanding book trade, and more opportunities for foreign travel facilitated the elite's introduction to the ideas of the Enlightenment. A selective reading of those ideas buttressed the disenchantment with Iberian rule and provided ready formulae for alternatives. The intellectuals flirted with a political ideology complementary to local rule, with economic ideas harmonious with free trade specifically, and with emerging capitalism generally. An inclination toward Physiocratic doctrine signified a willingness of part of the elites to continue the search for, as well as the exploitation and export of, raw materials—the continuation of a well-established pattern of thought and practice which argued poorly for economic independence.

Many of the intellectuals who questioned their Iberian experience while embracing various and sometimes contradictory Northern European examples held important governmental posts after political independence had been won from Spain and Portugal, while others occupied secondary but still influential positions in the nascent governments. They found ample opportunity to put their ideas and preferences into practice.[2]

Intensified contacts with Europe throughout the nineteenth century reaffirmed the conclusion reached by many of the elites familiar with the philosophies of the Enlightenment that the Europeans, particularly the English and French, had confected a desirable civilization worthy of emulation. The opinion of José Avelino Aramayo, a Bolivian visitor to the continent in 1877, that Europe not only represented progress but was needed to foment a similar progress in the New World, typified the thought of most of the elites. Aramayo did not hesitate to praise those Latin American nations which seemed most nearly to duplicate Europe.[3] In truth, Europe's rapid industrialization and technological change awed most of the impressionable Latin American cosmopolites, who clamored to replicate the process in their own locality, to graft the novelties on the quite different political, social, and economic institutions and realities of the New World. The effort to acquire the outward or material manifestations of the "progress" they acknowledged as civilization meant that, for these Latin Americans in the nineteenth century, progress could be measured quantitatively by the amount of exports, the number of steam engines, railroad miles, or gas lights. The more the capital city architecturally resembled Paris, then *ipso facto* the greater the degree of progress the country could claim.

The ideology of progress in nineteenth-century Latin America was nowhere better expressed than by the vocal Generation of 1837 in Argentina. Perhaps the intellectuals composing that generation achieved a greater cogency in their writing because they felt they faced a powerful alternative to their preferences in the caudillo Juan Manuel de Rosas, who dominated Argentina from 1829 until 1852. The members of the Generation of 1837 regarded their conflict with Rosas as a struggle between "civilization" and "barbarism," the dichotomy repeatedly invoked by Latin American intellectuals throughout the century. In defining civilization, the Generation of 1837 identified the Argentina they intended to create —and in fact did create—as a copy of Europe. In doing so, the members of that generation fastened on Argentina ideas, thought patterns, and prejudices which still remain.

Associated with the port of Buenos Aires, the members of that literary generation looked with horror on the rest of the nation as a vast desert in need of the civilizing hand of Europe. Buenos Aires would serve, according to their blueprint, as a funnel through which European culture would pass on its civilizing mission to redeem the countryside—if it was redeemable. Many of the elite finally concluded it was not and advocated European immigration as the best means to "save" Argentina. In accordance with the political views of the times, those elites aspired to govern Argentina by means of a highly restricted democracy. Esteban Echeverría summed up that aspiration in his *Dogma socialista* (1838):

Collective reason alone is sovereign, not the collective will. This will is blind, capricious, irrational: the will desires; reason examines, weighs, and decides. Thus it happens that the sovereignty of the people can reside only in the reason of the people, and that only the prudent and rational part of the social community is called to exercise that sovereignty. Those who are ignorant remain under the tutelage and safeguard of the laws decreed by the common consent of the men of reason. Democracy, then, is not the absolute despotism of the masses or of the majority; it is the rule of reason.[4]

That statement well represented elitist political thought, whether of that generation or later and, for that matter, whether of Argentina or elsewhere in Latin America. Some decades later, as a further example, the Bolivian Félix Avelino Aramayo advocated an aristocratic government "in the Greek sense of the word," "for" the people but not "by" the people.[5] The experienced and intelligent would be expected to govern for the greatest benefit of the nation, an ideology complementary to the earlier beliefs summarized by Echeverría. Nothing extraordinary resided in the concept of the few governing the many, but still it could prove devastating if the few challenged or changed, intentionally or not, the preferred life-styles of the many, and/or if by miscalculation the few lowered the quality of life of the majority.

Beyond the confines of the Generation of 1837, the *Dogma socialista* achieved neither the acclaim nor the influence of *Civilización y barbarie: Vida de Juan Facundo Quiroga* by Domingo Faustino Sarmiento. First published in 1845 in Chile, where the future Argentine president resided in exile, the book ranks as a major classic of Argentine literature. It also influenced generations of Latin Americans.[6] Emperor Pedro II of Brazil acknowledged to Sarmiento the importance he attributed to it.[7] The book denounced a major provincial caudillo, Juan Facundo Quiroga, who symbolized for Sarmiento to the worst "barbarism" of the vast interior of Argentina. The author forcefully set forth the dialectic so dear to the hearts of the Generation of 1837: the progress of the Europeanized city and ignorance, barbarism, and primitivism of the countryside. The gaucho folk society repulsed Sarmiento, who observed at one point, "The nineteenth century and the twelfth century coexist, the one in the cities; the other in the countryside."[8] Revealing a general schizophrenia notable in the works of most nineteenth-century Latin American intellectuals, parts of the book can be interpreted as sympathetic portraits of rural life and of the typical gaucho types: the track-finder, the pathfinder, the poet, and the outlaw. Still, Sarmiento could not accept the rural populations as the desirable national prototype. He denounced them for supporting the local caudillos whom they found representative. If they refused to accept the civilization of Europe, then, Sarmiento advised, European immigrants must repopulate Argentina.[9] Indeed, in his last book, *Conflictos y armonías de las razas en América* (1883), he demonstrated that he had imbibed the racist doctrines of nineteenth-century European social scientists to conclude that a racially mixed population doomed Argentina. All the more reason, therefore, to cleanse it with "superior" European blood. Sarmiento represented an extreme but not unusual position among his generation by affirming his willingness to bypass adaptation of European models for Argentina in favor of an exact recreation of Europe in Argentina. Those forceful and influential theses of Sarmiento were neither original nor isolated in the Americas. A year prior to the publication of the Argentine's rural-urban dialectic, for example, Francisco Bilbao published in Santiago his own analysis of Chilean society, *Sociabilidad chilena*, which equated the countryside with tradition and the cities with progress.[10]

The best-known Argentine novel of the nineteenth century, *Amalia*, further propagated those attitudes of the Generation of 1837.[11] Considered by many a prototype of Argentine Romanticism, it appeared first in serialized form; the complete novel was published in 1855. Its author, José Mármol, castigated the caudillo Rosas as a tyrant, the fitting representative of rural barbarism. The main protagonists are drawn from the capital's aristocracy, European in dress, thought, and action, in sharp contrast with the rustic supporters of the caudillo, who are depicted as the incarnation of evil. Further, an open racism characterizes the novel: the persecuted aristocracy is white, thus of pure European lineage and obviously "civilized"; the supporters of Rosas are a disagreeable and cruel lot of "mongrels": mulatto, mestizo, or racially mixed in one way or another and of course equated with inferiority and barbarism. *Amalia*, like *Civilización y barbarie* and *Dogma socialista*, represented the outlook and mentality of a generation instrumental in the shaping of Argentina in the nineteenth century. Indeed, two participants in that movement, Bartolomé Mitre and Sarmiento, served successively as presidents of Argentina, 1862–1868 and 1868–1874, crucial years in the formation of that nation.

The interplay of countryside and city absorbed the attention of the Latin American *literati*, who frequently made it a theme of their novels and stories. Accelerating urbanization was, after all, a major trend of the century, but also the association of the city with progress was inevitable. The Chilean novelist Alberto Blest Gana treated perceptively the interplay of rural and urban cultures in his *Martín Rivas* (1862). The young Rivas, innocent, even Puritanical, leaves the provinces for the city, where he is changed, "civilized" as it were. Blest Gana may picture the nobility of the countryside, but it still remains rustic; the city may appear corrupt, but it radiates culture. Subtly tracing the Europeanization of the virtuous Rivas, the novel depicts what appeared to the novelist and the reading public at the time as both inevitable and desirable.

The intellectuals did not have to be hostile to local or native American cultures to advocate Europeanization of the New World. Their own Europeanization blinded most of them to any alternatives. The Peruvian novelist Clorinda Matto de Turner exemplified this group. Her *Aves sin nido* (1889), widely acclaimed as the first novel in defense of the Indians, denounced in convincing prose the abuse and exploitation of the Peruvian Indians. She expressed her reasons for writing the novel as four: to call attention to the suffering of the Indians, to urge the reform of backward conditions in the Peruvian interior, to suggest the progress which must be made, and to help create a Peruvian literature.[12] Appropriately, in the preface to the third edition (1889), Emilio Gutiérrez de Quintanilla considered a major theme of *Aves sin nido* to be "civilization versus barbarism." Whereas the Spaniards should have introduced civilization in the Andes, they were responsible for enslaving and debasing the Indians, returning them to "the barbarism of the primitive past."[13] The Republic had the responsibility of redeeming the Indians through "education, employment, and equality."[14] Neither de Quintanilla nor Matto de Turner suggested that the Indians might find redemption through recourse to traditional native culture; both writers recommended a Europeanized future for them.

For Matto de Turner, the city symbolized the civilization needed to regenerate Peru. More than one inhabitant of the remote village of Killac affirms that the future lies in the city. As the character Manuel remarks in *Aves sin nido*, "All those who have sufficient means migrate to the centers of civilization."[15] Lima is presented in the novel as such a center. Speaking to two young girls on their way to the Peruvian capital for the first time, Manuel enthuses, "Oh yes, Lima! There the heart becomes educated and the mind instructed. . . . To travel to Lima is to go to heaven's antechamber and to see from there the throne of the Glory of the Future. They say that our beautiful capital is a fairytale city."[16] If one could move on to a European city the satisfaction would increase. Fernando Marín promises to take his wife from Killac to Lima and then caps his promise with the announcement that from there they will visit Europe.[17] A train transports those villagers from the rural past to the urban future. Fittingly, the train's engineer is an Englishman.

While Matto de Turner vividly denounced the barbarity of village life and graphically portrayed the injustices inflicted on the Indians, she was vague in offering solutions to end the debasement of the Indians other than migration to Lima, a solution which resolved few if any problems for millions of Indians over the centuries. She expressed a firm and typical, although ill-defined, hope that some answers would be provided by education, the most universally preferred solution since the Enlightenment, and evinced a general vagueness that somehow "pure Christianity"—never defined but certainly intended to be the opposite of the corrupt Catholicism she denounced in the novel—would uplift the Peruvians. Of course the religion Matto de Turner preferred was European in origin just as the education she advocated would inculcate the finest European values. Thus both religion and education would guarantee the cultural genocide of the majority. The conclusion deduced from the novel was that, if Europe had debased the Indians, Europe would also redeem them.[18] In her refusal to find any local solutions and her insistence on Europeanization of the Incas, Matto de Turner resembled Sarmiento. Although nearly half a century separated *Aves sin nido* from *Civilización y barbarie*, the ideology advocating European solutions to local problems in both books coincided. On the other hand, a major difference, and it is a significant one, separated the philosophy of the two: Matto de Turner blamed Europe for the "barbarization" of the Incas just as she believed Europe would "civilize" them.

The schizophrenia characteristic of the nineteenth-century intellectuals and consequently of their nationalism was acutely apparent in a writer-philosopher of the stature of Euclides da Cunha. His masterpiece, *Os sertões* (1902), admirably translated into English as *Rebellion in the Backlands*, ranks as a major classic in Latin American literature, worthy of a place of honor in world literature. Comte, Darwin, Spencer, and a host of other European mentors left their mark on da Cunha, who faithfully included their ideas in his analysis. Yet his book revealed a subtle questioning of those European theories, a daring stance for a Latin American intellectual at the end of the nineteenth century. Indeed, da Cunha's mind must have been a turmoil of struggle between sacrosanct European theory and his own perceptive observations of Brazil, so much so that in a later edition of his book he added some extraordinary footnotes indicating his inclination more toward observation of Brazil and thus away from exotic European theories.

As a journalist, da Cunha accompanied the federal army

into the *sertão*, the backlands, of Bahia in 1897 on the army's mission to exterminate the defiant followers of the religious mystic Antônio Conselheiro. That complex figure emerged on one level as a leader of the millenarian movement of awesome potential, and on another level he can be interpreted as an activist populist leader urging the poor to refuse to pay the new taxes levied on them by a distant government. He came to exercise a political, economic, and religious power whose appeal to the masses unnerved the elites. The state and federal governments, as well as the religious hierarchy, regarded him and his settlement at Canudos as a threat to be eliminated promptly. The expeditions to accomplish that goal represented the cities in their determination to subdue the countryside. A comfortable life in the cities near the coast did not prepare da Cunha for what he witnessed in the interior. The different types of people, customs, topography, even the differently spoken Portuguese astounded him. He felt that he had been transported "outside Brazil." The existence of "two societies" within a single nation caused him to reflect at great length on which was the real Brazil. He resolved his perplexity in favor of the poor but strong people of the hinterlands, whom he eventually classified as "the very core of our nationality, the bedrock of our race." He characterized their society as "the vigorous core of our national life."[19] For da Cunha the shock of discovering a new and different Brazil never dissipated. Some years after the publication of the first edition of *Os sertões*, obviously after much reflection and no little agony, he reinforced his previous conclusions:

I did encounter in the backlands type an ethnic subcategory already formed and one which, as a result of historical conditions, had been freed of the exigencies of a borrowed civilization such as would have hindered its definitive evolution. This is equivalent to saying that in that indefinable compound—the Brazilian—I came upon something that was stable, a point of resistance reminiscent of the integrating molecule in the initial stage of crystallization. And it was natural enough that, once having admitted the bold and inspiring conjecture that we are destined to national unity, I should have seen in those sturdy caboclos [backlanders] the hardy nucleus of our future, the bedrock of our race. . . .

. . . As we make our way deeper into the land . . . the pure white, the pure Negro, and the pure Indian are now a rarity. The generalized miscegenation, meanwhile, has given rise to every variety of racial crossing; but, as we continue on our way, these shadings tend to disappear, and there is to be seen a greater uniformity of physical and moral characteristics. In brief, we have struck bedrock—in the man of the backlands.[20]

Da Cunha's discovery disturbed most of the educated public, which still clung to its revered European images.[21]

Da Cunha found himself in an agonizing dilemma over his admiration for the people of the interior and his European indoctrination. *Os sertões* weakened—although it consistently adhered to realism—when the author resolved that the city must triumph over the countryside, Europeanization over Brazilianization. He proposed education as a weapon more powerful than cannons to subjugate the rebellious backlanders to the city. He found the justification for the war, then, to be the mission to carry civilization into the hinterlands. At one point he wrote:

The entire campaign would be a crime, a futile and a barbarous one, if we were not to take advantage of the paths opened by our artillery, by following up our cannon with a constant, stubborn, and persistent campaign of education, with the object of drawing these rude and backward fellow countrymen of ours into the current of our times and of our national life. . . . Our biological evolution demands the guarantee of social evolution. We are condemned to civilization. Either we shall progress or we shall perish. So much is certain and our choice clear.[22]

Thus, for all its nationalism and insight, *Os sertões* finally aligned itself with the forces of Europeanization. Da Cunha was a Social Darwinist who understood that the people of the interior, victims of aggression and injustice, must succumb to the advance of "progress." By supporting the city as civilization over the countryside as barbarity, *Os sertões* in the final analysis bore a close relationship to *Civilización y barbarie*, although perhaps da Cunha maintained an ambivalence uncharacteristic of Sarmiento.[23]

It was not the urban-rural dichotomy alone which preoccupied most of da Cunha's contemporaries. They viewed the question of civilization versus barbarism in racial terms also and subscribed to the European racial doctrines of the day which ranked the Aryan and Anglo at the pinnacle of civilization, while regarding the Africans and Indians as real obstacles to progress. A mixture of the European with either the Indian or black was regarded—as European social doctrine prescribed—as a sure condemnation to an inferior status. A leading cultural review published in Rio de Janeiro in 1895 castigated the Brazilian "race," composed of the "backward" African, "decadent" Portuguese, and "primitive" Indian. The author's recommendation was standard for the times: "What we need is new forces, originating in the strong and vigorous races which on arrival here will work by absorption to improve our race."[24] The Brazilian intellectuals put great faith in the "bleaching process," the eradication of the "weak" Indian and African genes by the "stronger," more "dominant" European ones. The theory may not have squared with European anthropological thought, but it provided a necessary solution for the distraught Brazilian elite and, according to its proponents, offered the surest method to reproduce European civilization in their vast nation.[25] Holding views harmonious with similar hopes in Argentina and elsewhere, the Brazilian intellectuals despaired of remolding the local populations, and so planned to replace them.

The intellectuals of Indo-America demonstrated no greater understanding or tolerance of the Indians than their Brazilian counterparts did of the Africans. The huge Indian populations of Mexico, Guatemala, Ecuador, Peru, Bolivia, and Paraguay embarrassed the intellectuals, who regarded them as barbaric at worst and as childlike creatures at best. The Indians' disdain of European civilization only intensified the suspicions of the intellectuals. Governments and landowners felt perfectly correct in forcing the Indians to labor for them under the rationalization that labor fostered contact with the elite and thus exposed the Indians to the indubitable benefits of European civilization. Whatever their professed political suasion, the Latin American elite seldom shied away from exploiting the Indians.[26]

The Mexican intellectuals vigorously debated the "Indian problem" in the nineteenth century, a debate which accelerated during the long government of Porfirio Díaz (1876–1911), whose policies divested the Indian communities of several million acres and literally enslaved entire Indian groups. The intellectuals divided over the intelligence and ability of the Indians as well as the feasibility of integrating them into national life, that is, making Europeanized Mexicans of the indigenous inhabitants. One side emphasized the potential of the Indians and urged the government to improve their conditions. Intellectuals like Justo Sierra believed that education and greater exposure to European ways, while rescuing the Indians, would transform them into mestizo Mexicans. To others, however, the Indians constituted an insuperable obstacle to national progress; these intellectuals particularly decried the Indians' communal spirit and lack of individualism. Writing in the 1860s, Antonio García Cubas identified the Indians as the "enemy" of other Mexicans and predicted that their "decadence and degeneration" could not be reversed. Decades later, Francisco Bulnes, the quintessential Social Darwinist, published his blunt and influential *El porvenir de las naciones hispano-americanas* (1899), which concluded that the racial inferiority of the Indians prohibited national development. The almost universally proposed solution to the "Indian problem" was the encouragement of European immigration with the hope that the new blood would dilute the Indian. The debates focused exclusively on whether or not the Indians could be Europeanized.[27] The intellectuals saw no alternative. None recognized that the Indians might want to draw on their own past rather than Europe's, and none perceived any attributes in the Indian communities worthy of incorporation into the national ethos.

The ideology apparent in the writings of most intellectuals from Sarmiento to da Cunha, and in almost all the governments of nineteenth-century Latin America, bore a variety of names: progress, civilization, development, and, retrospectively, modernization. Whatever the name applied, the idea was as constant as it was simple: to copy those aspects of Northern European—and, later, United States—culture which most struck the fancy of the elites, thus creating an imperfect and selective process of remolding their nations after foreign models.[28] Although technology appealed the most to the elites, they also aped certain life-styles and professed the values accompanying them. The intent of the elites was to graft onto Latin America the accouterments of progress rather than to accommodate new ideas and modes by reforming the basic national institutions. Thus modernization was pursued without changing such things as the hoary labor systems. The abolition of slavery was as much a convenience for the landowners as a humanitarian act, and the slaves were integrated promptly into other old and iniquitous labor practices. Railroads, to offer another example, became the symbol *par excellence* of progress, while at the same time they accelerated the expansion of the already well-institutionalized latifundia, further shifted the economy toward the export sector, and thus contributed to deepening dependency. More often than not the old elites succeeded in co-opting the potential leaders of the nascent urban middle class, which identified its goals more with upper-class life-styles than with meaningful reform of old institutions.

Throughout Latin America by the end of the nineteenth century the concept of progress as the emulation of Northern Europe and the United States triumphed. Ideological lines which once divided the elites blurred as the rural patriarchal elite fell under the influence and control exercised by banks, governmental regulations, marketing realities, and in general the increasingly more aggressive urban elites. Indeed, the sons of that once dominant rural patriarchy passed through the universities to become the doctors, lawyers, engineers, and bureaucrats of the Europeanized sector. The ruling minority relegated the majority, composed mainly of Indians, blacks, mulattoes, and mestizos, to marginal societal positions. While the countryside was regarded as hopelessly backward, the ruling—and increasingly urban—elites tolerated it, realizing that to tamper with the basic rural institutions would threaten a system which, if not perfect, still could be manipulated to favor the elites. At any rate, the capital cities with their cafés, theaters, operas, balls, academies, governmental intrigue, and Beaux Arts architecture absorbed the attention of the elite and to an ever larger degree symbolized their nations to them.

## An Elite Counterpoint

From the ranks of some intellectuals a warning sounded to beware of the uncritical aping of Northern Europe and the United States. They cautioned that modernization should proceed more slowly, and be mediated with Iberian and American values, or they countenanced other choices, alternatives put forth, advocated, defended, but defeated. These intellectuals' positions merit scrutiny, since they constitute possible solutions to problems Latin America confronted in the past century and in most cases still faces in the twentieth. Their caution assumes further significance as an expression, not always well formulated, of political, cultural, and/or economic nationalism, a force to be reckoned with in the twentieth century.

The deepening dependency of Latin America evident after mid-century alarmed an increasing number of the intellectuals and prompted them to avert their eyes from Europe to reexamine national reality. They began to perceive that the brand of "progress" their governments endorsed was at best cosmetic and at worst an instrument of imperialism perpetuating their subordination to Europe. That realization posed new questions.

Typical of their growing concern was the observation of Colonel Alvaro Gabriel Barros, an Argentine military figure and intellectual who had had extensive experience administering the bureaucracy of the governing elite:

In order to avert or cure the ills produced by the present crisis, we have recourse to and study analogous situations in other nations of the world. Once informed of what was done there with success, we take pleasure in implementing their solutions here, certain they will have similar results. We do not take the opportunity or time to study our own country to verify if the conditions are the same here or if the causes which have given rise to the crisis are similar.

These remarks revealed a disappointment with those intellectuals who knew far more about distant cultures than about their own national reality. Barros went on to criticize their concept of "progress" as one detrimental to the nation and beneficial to Europe:

The advantages of the railroad lines, the telegraphic network, the artificial ports, etc., will be real and great when such works respond to the needs of our progress, increased production, and enrichment. To invest in their acquisition huge amounts of capital with guaranteed interest as a means of progressing and enriching ourselves when at the same time we permit terrible and powerful agents actively working to exploit our riches is to ensure prosperity for other nations while acquiescing in our own ruin. They come here to crush us beneath their enormous weight.[29]

Barros exemplified a sharpening challenge from the intellecions of European dicta. The challenge revealed a growing preoccupation with local socioeconomic reality, a reversal of the previous romanticization of the environment. It served as a springboard for a new nationalism.

Fittingly, an intellectual once associated with the Generation of 1837, Juan Bautista Alberdi, began by the mid-1850s to question his peers' concept of "progress" and blind acceptance of European values. Alberdi's loyalty to his own federalist convictions first had prompted him to leave the Argentina of Rosas in 1838 and then had precipitated his break with Mitre and Sarmiento in 1853. For the remaining thirty-one years of his life, Alberdi criticized the program of the men who advocated the rapid modernization of Argentina. He boldly questioned the premise of those who would unquestioningly copy Europe in his denunciation of Sarmiento's *Civilización y barbarie* as invalid.[30] He asserted that "Characterizing the cities as civilized and the countryside as barbarian is an error of judgment and history."[31] The urban educated classes had behaved far more barbarously than the country folk, reasoned Alberdi:

There exists an educated barbarism a thousand times more disastrous for true civilization than that of all the savages of the American hinterlands. . . . The educated barbarians of the cities have eclipsed the rural caudillos with their wars twice as long, twice as bloody, twice as costly and disastrous as those of Rosas and Quiroga. Neither of those barbarians contracted loans for sixty millions of hard pesos, allowed the public debt to absorb half the national budget with interest payments, levied taxes higher than those paid in England, or allowed insecurity to reign in the city and countryside alike. . . .[32]

Contradicting the Sarmiento thesis, Alberdi argued that rural areas produced the nation's wealth, that the country folk had liberated Argentina from Spain, and that the countryside and the gaucho represented civilization.[33] "Civilization is neither gas nor steam nor electricity as those who are impressed with exterior appearances like to think," he wrote.[34] He defined Argentine civilization in these terms:

If there is a part of Argentina which by its geographical and natural conditions represents civilization it is that region composed of green, well-watered, flat, and fresh fields on which millions of animals roam. . . . The horse is another instrument and natural symbol of Argentine civilization, as worthy as the river, canal, or railroad. . . . But the horse is a useless machine without a skilled mechanic to operate it, which is to say without the gaucho who in this sense represents civilization in Argentina. . . . Our fields and our farmers cannot be classified as barbaric except in books written by someone who does not know what civilization is.[35]

Alberdi assigned "progress" a new meaning, at least a novel one in Latin America. While the Generation of 1837 equated progress with the copying of Europe, Alberdi believed it meant improving Argentina to meet national needs through the use of national resources and means.[36] It was a logical conclusion, which made "progress" a relative and not an absolute concept.

Alberdi's defense of the countryside coincided with the emergence of gaucho-inspired literature, a genre inspired by the folk tales and poems popular among the people of the pampas. It recognized the importance and legitimacy of local sources, vocabulary, themes, and style for literature. In 1872, José Hernández, long an astute social critic who understood the difference between growth and development, published the first part of his magnificent epic poem *Martín Fierro*; the

second part came out in 1879. Bristling with sharp social protest, the verses exalted the gaucho, whose nobility contrasted
sharply with the villainy of the urban politician. The purity of
the countryside had been polluted; injustice masqueraded as
civilization. The poem sounded the call for a new caudillo to
save the people:

> For me, the tail is tenderloin
> and spine is filet,
> I'll make my nest wherever I am
> and eat whatever I find;
> I'll go around meek as a lamb
> and knock on any door.
>
> And I'll let the ball roll on,
> since some day it's got to stop;
> a gaucho has to put up with things
> until that hole in the ground swallows him up,
> or until some real man comes along
> to take over out here.[37]

While the Argentine literary establishment dismissed the poem, it enjoyed unprecedented popular success, going through
edition after edition of thousands of copies each. The people
obviously saw in the poem a truth, a vindication which appealed to them. They identified with it, something they were
unable to do with the standard Europeanized literature of the
elite.

Eduardo Gutiérrez also praised the gaucho. The plot of his
novel *Juan Moreira*—first serialized in a newspaper in 1879–
1880—turned on a theme similar to that of Hernández: the
hard-working gaucho as a victim of an unjust society. In 1886,
the novel was dramatized to enthusiastic public acclaim.
Drama historians consider its production as the origin of the
national theater.

As gaucho literature emerged, a few historians began to
take a different perspective on the past in the first, timid challenge to the standard interpretations of Bartolomé Mitre, Vicente Fidel López, and Domingo Faustino Sarmiento, authors

who had lauded foreign influence and discredited the aspirations of the people outside of Buenos Aires. The historical controversy which followed centered on the figure of the caudillo Juan Manuel de Rosas, who, during more than two decades of power, had defied the Europeans, withstood French and English blockades, held a tight reign on the local elite, and enjoyed a genuine popularity among the masses. When Adolfo Saldías published his three-volume *Historia de Rosas y su época* (1881/1884/1887) and Ernesto Quesada his *La época de Rosas* (1898), they brought into question some of the elitist prejudices which had clouded the perspective of generations of historians who routinely damned Rosas, conceding only that he had been the most powerful and successful of the "barbaric" caudillos. The new studies suggested a reconsideration of the past which would give added weight to native—as opposed to European—values and thereby assign Rosas a key nationalist role. They set in motion a heated debate which still rages over the significance of Rosas in Argentine history.[38] Some of the most recent revisionist examinations of nineteenth-century Argentina conclude that genuine national development took place during the Rosas years, while deepening dependency characterized the nation's fate during the remaining half-century.[39]

After 1865 some Brazilian writers began to examine their own nation more critically. Not surprisingly, that concern involved them in national crises shaking the once-somnolent empire. A new bourgeoisie, taking shape as the cities grew in size, felt strong enough to challenge the old rural oligarchy for power. The expensive and long war with Paraguay, 1864–1870, the rise of republican sentiment, and abolitionist campaigns which challenged the institution of slavery excited debate and prompted the rise and fall of several governments. Those crises stimulated literary production and were in turn aggravated by social criticism from the *literati*, who increasingly occupied themselves with questions of national self-examination.

Sílvio Romero was one of the most skillful analysts of Brazil. He wrote prolifically, but no work exceeds in importance his monumental *História da literatura brasileira* (1888).

Of lasting value, it remains as essential for an understanding of Brazil today as when it was first published. Romero considered literature as a national expression and an integral part of society, an inescapable conclusion in Brazil, where the *literati* played multiple roles in society. He lamented that Brazilian literature and history had placed excessive emphasis on the elite to the neglect of the people, whom he considered the basic force of society. In an effort to relate the masses and literature, he published two anthologies of folk poems and songs: *Contos populares do Brasil* (1885) and *Estudos sobre a poesia popular do Brasil* (1888). Although he had to deal with European racist doctrine which influenced and would continue to influence so many Brazilian intellectuals, he boldly proclaimed that Brazil was not the exclusive product of Europe but the joint effort of Indians, Europeans, and Africans— a truly revolutionary thought at the time. Romero was the first Brazilian intellectual to accord the blacks their just position alongside the other races in the construction of Brazil. He had a vision of the future as well as of the past. He understood a reality which still eludes most: Before Brazil could develop, it would be necessary to reform basic agrarian institutions by abolishing slavery and redistributing the land. Such a realistic blueprint for the future required fundamental changes which the elite stubbornly resisted. True, slavery was abolished in 1888, only to be replaced with insidious forms of debt peonage which neither altered the quality of life of the rural masses, nor changed the land ownership patterns, nor loosened the tight noose of dependency. Instead of a wider distribution of land, the succeeding generations witnessed an even greater concentration of land in fewer and fewer hands. Romero correctly observed, as did José Hernández in La Plata,[40] that agrarian reforms were basic to any effort to modernize and develop Brazil and to create a rational society.

Although himself under the influence of European ideologies of his day, Romero attempted to free himself so that he could see his own country through Brazilian eyes. Seemingly, he resolved the perennial intellectual dilemma more successfully than Euclides da Cunha. The perceptive da Cunha was to conclude that Europeanization was inevitable. Along the complex spectrum ranging from Americanism to Europeanism, he placed himself, however reluctantly, closer to Europeanism than did Romero, who forcefully condemned blind imitation of Europe and called for intellectual independence. Romero aimed his critical barbs at "the figure of the imitator, of the slavish and witless copier of each and every trifle that the ships from Portugal or France or any other place bring us."[41] Advocating national introspection, he crusaded for a Brazilian literature with its roots in the people, one which would interpret the national environment, traditions, and sentiments. The major obstacle to such national expression, he concluded, was that "we do not know ourselves."[42]

Brazil's most perceptive historian, João Capistrano de Abreu, began to write at approximately the same time as Romero, and his message was much the same: Brazilian culture in its imitation of European modes was not expressive of the national soul. This imitative culture, isolated from its own environment, did not represent the "conscious expression of the people."[43] Capistrano de Abreu revolutionized historical studies in Brazil by turning attention from the coastal band, with its obvious link to Europe, and examining the previously little-known interior. He presented his major thesis in 1889 in a short but brilliant essay, *Os caminhos antigos e o provoamento do Brasil*, the single most important statement on Brazilian history yet made. Neglecting the archbishops, generals, and viceroys who had populated the histories of Brazil to that date—even refusing to treat the official national hero, Tiradentes, whom he considered more the creation of the elite than a representation of the Brazilian people—he concentrated on the contributions of the masses, the meaningful periodization of the past, and significant themes in Brazilian history. He wrote:

. . . In history we only point to the dominant figures, those who destroyed or constructed, leaving behind a trail of blood or a ray of hope. We do not remember the shoulders which bore them, or the courage of the masses which gave them their strength, the collective mind which exalted their minds, the unknown hands which pointed out to them the ideal which only the most fortunate attained. And often the unknown person is the one whose cooperation was most vital in bringing about the great event.[44]

If the masses made history, it was the vast interior which constituted the true Brazil, the valid national reality. Only when the coastal inhabitants turned their backs on the sea and penetrated the interior did they shed their European ways and become Brazilianized. Capistrano de Abreu's *Caminhos antigos* contained a remarkable global vision of the Brazilian past which emphasized the themes of exploration and settlement of the interior, the creation of overland and fluvial transportation networks welding the vast nation together, and cultural diversity as well as the psychological changes wrought in the Brazilian people. Capistrano de Abreu focused attention on the national heartland and the people who opened and settled it.

Other intellectuals, scattered throughout the rest of Latin America, contributed their own insights which upheld local values and questioned the wisdom of further importing European civilization. The Venezuelan Ramón Ramírez can serve as an excellent example. While a professor at the University of Caracas, he published a fascinating political analysis, *El cristianismo y la libertad: Ensayo sobre la civilización americana* (1855).[45] "European civilization spawns materialism to the neglect of the spirit," Ramírez charged.[46] While interested in the inventions pouring out of the Old World, he concluded that material advancement had become an end in itself rather than a means to advance public well-being. He criticized the "democracy" being practiced in the Americas as the rule of the privileged few over the many. Because European civilization benefited the minority at the expense of the majority, the Americans must resist the temptation to copy Europe, the originator, after all, of the hemisphere's present problems, and create a new civilization of their own. Perhaps, he reasoned, the turmoil characteristic of Latin America since independence was the violent gestation of that new civilization. Not immune from European influences himself, Ramírez argued that the new American civilization should be based on the

Christian socialism he discussed at length in the second half of his book. All in all, he provided a useful analysis of the New World and suggested a well-argued alternative to the blind copying of Europe in vogue in Venezuela as in other parts of Latin America.

Compromised already, these intellectuals, although wary of Europeanization, mediated acceptance and a selective adaptation of European values and techniques. They understood the attraction of Europe, yet appreciated the American experience as well. Somewhat naïvely, perhaps, they sought to combine the best of both, and in that respect they represented a third position between a Europeanized society on the one extreme and a folk society on the other. In the last third of the century Ignacio Manuel Altamirano in Mexico and Joaquín V. González in Argentina perceived their ideal society to be rural, well-ordered, and patriarchal. Altamirano idealized a mountain village in his *La Navidad en las montañas* (1871). A simple but good place, the village boasted of happiness, a high morality, harmony, and a patriarchal society in which priest, mayor, school teacher, and village elders guided the local inhabitants. At the beginning of the short novel, the narrator comments, "I had promised myself that I would end my journey in a small village of poor, but hospitable mountaineers who lived from the product of the soil and who enjoyed a relative well-being, thanks to their isolation from large, populous centers and to the goodness of their patriarchal customs." On the final page, he has much the same to say: "I myself forgot all my troubles and felt happy, contemplating that picture of simple virtue, and true, modest happiness which in vain I had sought for in the midst of opulent cities and in a society agitated by terrible passions."[47] Nonetheless, "progress" had penetrated that mountain village. The priest had introduced new crops, trees, and animals. A small grinding mill had freed the women from the metate. The villagers had built a school and hired a teacher, who in turn played an important and influential role in mediating further progress. To González, in *Mis montañas* (1893), the rugged and quiet countryside with its noble people constituted the "real," the "original" Argentina. Interestingly enough, both Gonzáles and Sarmiento were from La Rioja province, which both described in their books. If Sarmiento denigrated both the province and the gaucho, González idealized them. If Sarmiento hailed progress, González revered tradition: "Tradition is also a force; it is created by the sentiment and passion of the social mass and by a community of interests; it is a historic and philosophic element which explains great events; it is the history of peoples who have no history, the customs of peoples who have no formal laws."[48] *Mis montañas*, like *La Navidad en las montañas* offered a quiet counterpart to the hosannas acclaiming Europeanization. They can be read as nostalgic but symbolic descriptions of an idealized rural society, quaint reminders of the past to the modernizers.

These debates of the intellectuals—the majority enamored with Europe, while a vociferous minority urged caution and occasionally offered alternatives—are easy to follow. The published views of the opponents are still readily available. Their discussions, although emotional at times, were more often than not carried on pacifically in the fashion of a formalized debating society. The views of some dissenters have been offered in this section to indicate philosophical divisions among the elites themselves, but it must be reemphasized that those dissenters constituted a minority. The socioeconomic process, which the majority of the intellectuals endorsed, prevailed.

The general philosophical harmony of nineteenth-century Latin American historiography has preserved for a long time the one-dimensional view of that century.[49] In the first place, shaped by the triumph of European ideas, that historiography treated the Americas almost exclusively as an extension of Europe. Relegating the Indian past to the anthropologists, "history" began with the arrival of the Iberian conquerors and followed the transfer and growth of Iberian institutions. In the second place—and as a corollary to the first—the historians came from the ranks of the upper class or were upwardly mobile, with aspirations to please and to enter that privileged class. Because of their own background, associations, and aspirations, as well as their historical concerns and sources, the historians more often than not accepted the national institutional structures and approved the activities of the elites, from whom they selected representatives for their biographies. The similarity they ascribed to the past harmonized more with a class vision than with the totality of experience.[50] That "ideology of class" rationalized the institutions and the elites who controlled them, a justification which helped legitimize both and contributed to their continuity. The values and goals of that ideology served the elites well as one effective means to coerce larger and larger segments of the population into accepting the institutional structures and social systems of Latin America, even though those structures and systems were more detrimental than beneficial to an overwhelming majority of the population. The historians contributed mightily to the creation of a sense and feeling of nationality, albeit one complementary to the interests of the elites. In doing so, they successfully shrouded national histories with a sacred mystique which has inhibited broader historical investigations and even ridiculed the posing of some fundamental historical questions which might cast doubt on the efficacy of "modernization," "progress," and "development," not to mention the national institutions themselves.

The exclusivity of Latin American historiography inhibited the discussion of alternatives to Europeanization, excepting, as previously mentioned, some of the debates among the intellectuals themselves. For example, once the elites returned to power in Buenos Aires in 1852, they set about not only to eliminate the populist caudillos in the interior and in neighboring Paraguay but also to write history complementary to their actions, the official textbooks which nurtured succeeding generations of Argentine schoolchildren. Bartolomé Mitre, both a prolific historian and an energetic president of the nation, subscribed fully to the elitist concept of Europe as the single source of civilization.[51] He believed that the educated minority made history and should impose its will on the ignorant masses.[52] On the one hand, as president, Mitre opened the doors to foreign penetration. On the other, as a historian, he shaped the past to suit his present ends. Leaders with whom he disagreed he simply erased from the pages of history or relegated to inferior or negative positions. He informed fellow historian Vicente Fidel López, "We have almost the same predilection for great men and the same repulsion for the barbarian troublemakers such as [José Gervasio] Artigas whom we have buried historically."[53] The task of disinterring what previous generations of historians have buried is not an easy one, and it is complicated by the fact that most of society never articulated in written form its complaints, alternatives, or activities.

## The Popular Voice

Few studies consider the popular alternatives to the modernization pursued by the elites. Historians' customary fascination with the privileged as well as a lack of conventional documentation for the alternatives explain the silence. Because the overwhelming majority of the nineteenth-century Latin Americans were illiterate, they left few written accounts of their complaints, alternatives to Europeanization, or, for that matter, activities. That paucity of conventional documentation complicates but should not impede the search for popular preferences. However, it will require primarily the mastery of new sources and secondarily a reinterpretation of some of the more standard ones.

José Luis Romero ranks as one worthy scholar who has attempted to come to grips with the popular alternatives to the politics of the dominant elite in nineteenth-century Argentina. While more sympathetic to the process of Europeanization in his study, *History of Argentine Political Thought*, he, nonetheless, devoted much more than the usual token discussion to the countercurrent. He termed the popular alternative "inorganic democracy," which he defined thus:

But for many reasons the provincials opposed the doctrinaire positions and the institutional principles of the enlightened group. To these ideas the people of the interior opposed a profoundly colonial mentality and local sentiments, by which they demonstrated their new-born patriotism. . . . The people chose to obey the call of the caudillos of their class and of their own kind who sprang up on all sides, which gave support to a new authoritarianism that had some vaguely democratic characteristics, since, in fact, the caudillo exalted the ideals of his people and carried to power with him a mandate to impose and defend their wishes. . . . The creoles were accustomed to the enjoyment of immense personal liberty. The desert assured them that freedom, although at the cost of their total exclusion from public life, which was run by the cities. When the revolutionary movement triumphed, the creoles wanted to transfer their feeling of indomitable liberty to political life, since mere obedience to laws appeared to them to be oppression. . . . From this unlimited sense of freedom was born a democratic desire to have their own chief rule.[54]

The rustic rurals described by Romero had evolved a life-style which provided them with greater equality, security, and well-being within their own informal institutions than did the European pattern being imposed by Buenos Aires. Novelists, such as Leopoldo Lugones in *La guerra gaucha* (1905), also have attempted to distill the essence of the meaning and function of those popular institutions, of which they intuitively approve. A 1942 Argentine film based on Lugones's novel and bearing the same title opened with a dedication to "Those Forgotten by History" and emphasized in the spirit of the novel that the harmony of the people with their geography forged the strength that defeated the Spaniards in the Argentine Andean region, 1814–1818, and guaranteed the independence of that interior region. The personification of those people was the caudillo Martín Güemes, revered by the humble mountain folk but held at arm's length by the official historians domiciled in the distant national capital. The mutual identification of people and caudillo exemplified the "inorganic democracy" which Romero found characteristic of the Argentine interior during much of the last century.

What Romero termed "inorganic democracy" can be related to "folk culture," a common way of life shared by the ordinary people, a general concept useful for the study of nineteenth-century Latin America.[55] What distinguished the folk of nineteenth-century Latin America was their adherence to ideas and values formulated by the American experience over centuries. While the folk drew cautiously and slowly from European sources, they did not embrace the values and ideol-

ogy emanating from Europe—and later from North America
—with the same enthusiasm and rapidity that generally characterized the elites, the wealthy, and the aspiring middle
class. The folk stratum found in both the rural and urban
communities composed the largest part of preindustrial Latin
American society. Imbued with long traditions, those folk
cultures had undergone a variety of changes and adaptations
over the centuries. To a greater or lesser degree, depending on
the region, they drew from the Indian experience. For millen-
nia, the Indians lived in hunting, fishing, gathering, agrarian,
and village settings, modified in large regions of the Americas
by the rise of kingdoms and empires and the attendant influence of the socioeconomic system of cities and villages. Still,
the Indian monarchs shared similar customs, traditions, and
values with their subjects; in blood they were one with the
people. Even after the trauma of the Spanish and Portuguese
conquests, there existed some degree of tolerance within Iberian institutions toward local customs, necessarily so in remote and marginal areas. Nonetheless, powerful Spanish and
Portuguese influences over the centuries reshaped the Indian
societies. Those influences were even more pronounced on
the Africans, who had been removed from their cultural en-
vironments. European peasant folk cultures were transferred
to the New World as well. As the new Latin American nations
took political shape in the first half of the nineteenth century,
the governments, largely European in spirit, confronted viable
folk cultures which had amalgamated Indian, African, and
European traditions. From the vantage point of the Europeanized elites of the capital cities, those folk cultures and specifically the folk societies—organized groups of individuals
characterized by a folk culture—stood as barriers to the creation of the desired "modern" state, an argument well summarized by Sarmiento.

Folk culture was based on a common language, heritage,
beliefs, and means of facing daily life. It instilled feelings of
unity, loyalty, and tradition within the folk, more intuitive
than codified, although folk wisdom, folk poetry, and folk
tales gave verbal insight into such feelings.

In the nineteenth century, particularly during the first

half, the folk culture thrived within folk societies in the countryside and in the rural villages. Those folk societies comprised small, isolated communities which manifested a strong sense of group solidarity. The common folk culture bound people together into an intradependent, intimate, and largely self-sufficient society—a well-defined moral order in which each person knew his role and the interrelationships of individuals characterized the folk society. That unity of feeling and action accompanied a sense of harmony with the environment to satisfy inner needs. The combination of unity, harmony, and satisfaction comprised the soul of the people.

Education within those societies emphasized the individual's relationship to the group and inculcated in children a moral behavior honored by the community. In short, the result was to recreate in the child the patterns of the adult. Education provided continuity by passing on and maintaining tradition.

The incentives to work and to trade originated in tradition, moral dictates, community obligations, and kinship relations. Economic decisions took second place to social considerations. The system worked sufficiently well to provide the folk with employment, food, housing, community spirit, and reasonable satisfaction. Life-styles were simple; hardships were common; the disadvantages were obvious, at least to the outsider. Such life-styles repulsed the Europeanized elites of the cities. Yet those folk societies seem to have provided adequately for their members. Modest as their standards of living may have been, they deteriorated under the accelerating modernization of the nineteenth century, which first modified and then partially eradicated the folk societies.[56]

An interplay between folk cultures and the Europeanizing cities always existed. Within the cities themselves, folk cultures, although not folk societies, thrived, characterized by a symbiotic Europeanization. Esteban Echeverría drew an unflattering portrait of the folk element of Buenos Aires in his novelette *La matadora* (written around 1838 but not published until 1871). Not surprisingly, that vocal member of the Generation of 1837 decried the urban folk as a threat to Europeanization. Under pressures from the Europeanized elites, who succeeded in effecting economic growth, urbanization, industrialization, and modernization in some parts of Latin America, the folk societies diminished, although the folk cultures, as in the past, accommodated to much of the change and continued to exist in forms distinct from those earlier in the century.

Some of the leaders selected by the folk played significant roles in regional and national life. The folk expected any leader to represent and strengthen their unity, express their soul, and increase their harmony, in short, to be as one with the people he led. Nineteenth-century history, particularly the first half, abounds with such leaders, often referred to as caudillos—although, of course, not all caudillos were folk leaders. The popularity of such caudillos is undeniable. Their governments rested on a base of folk culture, drew support and inspiration from the folk, and expressed, however vaguely, their style of living. Under the leadership of such caudillos, the masses felt far more identification with government than they ever did under the imported political solutions advocated by the intellectuals and the elites.[57] Juan Bautista Alberdi, more than anyone else in the nineteenth century, studied the psychology of the relationship of popular caudillos with the masses, and he concluded that the people regarded a popular caudillo as "guardian of their traditions," the defender of their way of life.[58] He insisted that such leaders constituted "the will of the popular masses. . . . the immediate organ and arm of the people . . . the caudillos are democracy." He reiterated frequently in his writing the equation of the popular caudillo with democracy:

Thus, the system of caudillos appears in America in the form of democracy and together they develop and progress. Artigas, López, Güemes, Quiroga, Rosas, Peñaloza, as chiefs, heads, and authorities are the product of the people, their most spontaneous and genuine personification. Without any other authorization than that, without finances, without resources, they have guided the people with more power than the governments possess.[59]

In his biography of Aparicio Saravia, Manuel Gálvez noted that Saravia's death in 1904, during his struggle against President José Batlle of Uruguay, the city, and foreign influence, marked the end of the era of the caudillo on horseback in the Americas. Gálvez tried to distill what Saravia represented and concluded that he personified gaucho liberty, Iberian and Roman Catholic tradition, nationalist sentiments, distrust of foreign influence, an order based on hierarchy, and respect for moral values. In short, Saravia incarnated what was Spanish and profoundly American in the Uruguayan people.[60] He well represented the not unusual alliance of folk and landlords who shared traditional rural values and were cautious of urban and foreign ways. Such alliances obviously crossed class lines, reemphasizing the cultural nature of this nineteenth-century conflict. The hazy class lines complicate the application of customary political labels to those alliances, since the folk favored community arrangements which might suggest a rustic socialism, while the landlords represented, depending on one's viewpoint, a type of neo-feudalism or patrimonialism or neo-capitalism.

Argentine history offers excellent examples of popular and populist caudillos: Juan Facundo Quiroga, Martín Güemes, and Angel Vicente Peñaloza, to mention only a few obvious ones. Certainly the caudillo of greatest import was Juan Manuel de Rosas, who, in one way or another, dominated Argentina from 1829 until 1852. The masses demonstrated their loyalty by their willingness to fight for him during nearly a quarter of a century. Rosas suffered defeat and exile only when the elites enlisted the Brazilian army to unite with them to overthrow him. The concepts of these caudillos as the popular leaders of the masses and of the mutual devotion of leader and masses were as difficult for most of the Europeanized elite to accept as were the popular leaders.[61] The identification of the masses with Rosas explains in part the negative role assigned that caudillo in official Argentine historiography as well as the historical obscurity to which a dozen local leaders have been banished.

Two other examples of the popular caudillo exercising national power were José Gaspar Rodríguez de Francia of Paraguay (1814–1840) and Rafael Carrera of Guatemala (1839–1865). Their governments rested solidly on a base of folk culture, drew support and inspiration from the people, and expressed, however vaguely, their style of life. The Indian majorities of Paraguay and Guatemala felt they benefited from such popular governments and identified with the governments of Francia and Carrera.

The sources for the study of an alternative history, that of the folk rather than the well-documented history of the elites, have survived to some degree in folklore. Argentine folklore, for example, including gaucho poetry, offers evidence of popular support for "inorganic democracy," with the local caudillos regarded as the defenders of the people's rights and preferences.[62] While praising the rustic virtues of the countryside, the folklore denigrated the cities, filled with foreigners and subject to European influences.[63] True, critics detect a defense of the neo-feudalism which to them characterized parts of the countryside, but another aspect of the rural area was the opportunity for the gaucho to acquire his own string of ponies and herd of cattle, thus demonstrating a social mobility and flexibility contrary to feudalism as well as unusual later under Argentine capitalism. Also, the great space and isolation of the pampas engendered freedom and individuality among the gauchos. Certainly until mid-century an informality of relationships existed in the pampas which the integration of Argentine beef and wheat into the world market later destroyed. Much of the pertinent folklore reminisces nostalgically about that informality.

The large Indian population of Latin America tenaciously resisted the efforts to Europeanize them. The Indians constituted a majority in fully a third of the nations during the nineteenth century and a sizable minority in many of the others. They showed every evidence of preferring their own customs to those of the distant metropolis or the isolated capital city and their communal life to the new nation-state. They refused to dress like Europeans.[64] While acknowledging Roman Catholicism, they often retained vestiges of their own religion, establishing a syncretism which in some cases infiltrated the European community. They participated in the local, not the national, economy. They revered their own values and ignored those radiating from Europe. In fact, they often juxtaposed their own wisdom and the official values. From the capital city may have reverberated through the constitution and laws such echoes of the Enlightenment as "All men are created equal," but local wisdom noted in proverbs, "For the rich who robs the garden there is no law, no judge, no prison; but if a poor man steals a crumb the thief goes to jail."[65] Brazilian folk narrative, derived from Ibero-Afro-Amerindian sources, identified the rich as "bad" and the society dominated by the wealthy as a "world apart" in which the poor could not hope to occupy anything but a subservient position.[66]

The Mexican *corridos* also commented on social distinctions, attacking the morals, habits, and dress of the elite. Significantly those corridos emphasized violence and thereby contributed to the conclusion that violence was one of the most notable characteristics of nineteenth-century Latin America. As an intricate part of Mexican life, "of, by, and for the *pueblo*," the corridos offer a magnificent insight into the popular mind as well as important historical documents for the study of the masses.[67] The otherwise elusive public opinion they preserve proves to be radically different from the better-known ideology of the elite. Apparently the folk poets were splendid representatives of the people.[68] Their poems provided a matrix of homogeneity and common identification for the masses over a broad geographic area, thereby imparting a solidarity comparable to the well-forged unity of the elites with their standardized ideology.[69]

Passive resistance often gave way to rebellion as the Indians demonstrated their willingness to defend their way of life from further inroads of Europeanization. Since official historiography has been reluctant to recognize popular wrath and to discuss the implications of it, little attention has been given to Indian resistance and alternatives. Guatemala provides a handy and useful example of Indian resistance and temporary success as well as the subsequent silence accorded it in the history texts.

At mid-century the population of Guatemala numbered less than a million. The overwhelming majority was Indian, nominally Roman Catholic, non-Spanish-speaking, and min-

imally influenced by three centuries of Spanish rule. The
Spaniards had respected much of the indigenous culture.
However, independence in 1821 elevated to power a segment
of the elite which had imbibed the heady wines of Enlightenment thought and, judging the Indians to be backward, termi-
nated the benign neglect of the Crown. According to the sim-
ile of the times, the Indian civilization marked the appropriate
infancy of Guatemala, which would mature to adulthood nurtured on a European diet.[70] In short, if Guatemala were to
progress, then the Indians had to be Europeanized.

During the decade of the 1830s, the government of Mari-
ano Gálvez energetically set out to remodel Guatemala in an
effort to eradicate Indian institutions in favor of the latest
European ones. As elsewhere in the hemisphere, the government favored European immigration as the guarantee for
progress. In a moment of generosity—or desperation—in
1834, the government awarded nearly all the public lands to
foreign companies which promised to people Guatemala with
Europeans. The area conceded covered nearly three-quarters
of Guatemala.[71] Regarding the Indian communal lands as an
unprogressive remnant of the past, the government proceeded
to put them up for sale, a bargain eagerly acquired by a growing and ambitious mestizo urban class as well as by foreigners.
New laws forced the Indians to build roads and ports and re-
established the burdensome head tax on them in order to finance the infrastructure which would integrate Guatemala
more completely with Europe. At every turn the Indians faced
increasingly heavy taxes and workloads, confiscation of their
lands, and deprecation of their cultural values. At the same
time the government intensified its attacks on the Roman
Catholic clergy as retrograde and legislated to reduce its influence. To the Indian communities, on the other hand, the
clergy remained as their last protector from a hostile, Europeanized government. They perceived any decrease in the
Church's powers as an increase in their own vulnerability to
exploitation or destruction.[72] Clearly, by debilitating the only
defender of the Indian masses, the elites enhanced their own
position. The elites understood the organizational strength of
the Roman Catholic Church to surpass that of the nascent

political institutions they fostered, and they welcomed the opportunity to weaken a rival. Furthermore, the property confiscated from the Church ended up in the hands of the secular elites and increased their wealth, their prestige, and ultimately their power. The many grievances of the Indians reached a climax in 1837 with the outbreak of a virulent cholera epidemic, the final proof to the Indians that the government sought to eliminate them in order to give their lands to immigrants. At that point a popular revolt, one of the major ones in nineteenth-century Latin America, broke out, and Rafael Carrera, a mestizo with firm roots in the Indian community, took the leadership.

Among the many things that popular rebellion signified, it voiced the refusal of the Indians to countenance any further exploitation and destruction through Europeanization. They wanted to be left alone by the elites of Guatemala City so that they could live unmolested according to the dicta of their own culture. They rejected the education, culture, economy, and laws which would Europeanize them to the extent of integrating them into a capitalist economy centered in Europe. They chose to withdraw, to isolate themselves; and withdrawal was and remains a common reaction of the Indians before the Europeans. But withdrawal signified rebellion in regions where the elites depended on those Indians for labor and taxes. Carrera understood the Indian position; he sympathized with the desires of the Indians; and he rose to power on their strength.

During the generation (1838–1865) in which Rafael Carrera dominated Guatemala, he respected the native cultures, protected the Indians insofar as that was possible, and sought to incorporate them into his government. His modest successes in these efforts assume greater significance when compared to the disastrous conditions suffered by the Indian majority during the decades of liberal, Europeanized governments which encapsulated the Carrera period. That popular caudillo, totally unschooled in foreign theories, was a practical man who knew Guatemala and its peoples well. He had traveled and lived in many parts of the nation, always among the humble folk whom he understood. He drew from his Guatemalan experiences, in marked contrast to the elites seduced by European experiences and theories. Carrera appreciated the Indians' opposition to the process of Europeanization imposed by the Liberals.[73] He regarded it as his principal duty to allow "the people to return to their customs, their habits, and their particular manner of living."[74] The government, he affirmed, had the obligation of representing the majority of the people and of offering "a living example of virtue, equity, prudence, and justice."[75] Those principles seem to have guided much of his long administration.

While Carrera repudiated the radical ideas of the Liberals, he never eschewed change. He believed it must come slowly and within the social context, a change acceptable to the people and not forced on them. An editorial in *El Noticioso* as late as 1861 decried the wholesale importation of innovations from Europe and the United States and went on to advocate the evolution from a colonial past to a national present with deliberation.[76] Such gradualism generally characterized the Guatemalan government under Carrera. Revisionist studies of those years credit that government with respecting Indian customs and protecting the rural Indians.[77] The president held that the art of governing well sprang from the "formation of a government of the people and for the people."[78] Accordingly, the government officially abandoned the Liberals' goal to incorporate the Indians into Western Civilization. One even could argue that under Carrera the government was "Indianized." Indians and particularly Ladinos, all of relatively humble classes, participated directly in the government, holding such exalted offices, in addition to the presidency, of course, as the vice-presidency, ministries, governorships, and high military ranks. The army became nearly an Indian institution.[79] The Carrera government was unique in Latin America for providing the political ascendancy of the once conquered race. Significantly the "white" political monopoly was broken, and never again could the minute white aristocracy govern Guatemala alone.[80] Fundamental to Carrera's government was the decree of August 16, 1839, to protect the Indians.[81] Commenting on the new decree, *El Tiempo* editorialized, "It is the object of public interest not only to protect the most numerous class in our society but also to encourage it to improve its customs and civilization, which can be done by providing it with the means to acquire and increase its small property holdings and the industry by which it lives."[82] Such were the intentions of the Carrera government.

The government generally succeeded in carrying out those intentions. Governmental decrees were translated into Indian languages and "protectors" appointed to serve the Indian communities. Carrera himself received Indian delegations and seems to have traveled frequently in order to visit with the Indians.[83] To lift some of the economic burden from the impoverished majority, he reduced taxes on foodstuffs and abolished the head tax. Further, he excused the Indians from contributing to the loans the government levied from time to time to meet fiscal emergencies. On the other hand, the government did not hesitate to reinstate the former alcoholic beverage controls, which included higher taxation, one means Carrera had of both increasing revenues and imposing a greater morality on the countryside.[84] The government took a pragmatic view toward education. It encouraged a basic education, believing that for the majority of the inhabitants a simple education emphasizing reading, writing, and Christian doctrine would suffice. Higher education was available, primarily in the capital, for those desiring it.[85] In the almost exclusively Indian Department of Sacatepequez, a decree of 1849 required each village to establish a school for boys to learn reading, writing, arithmetic, religion, and moral principles. "As soon as funds are available, those municipalities will establish schools for girls." Scholarships were to be available to defray expenses of poor children.[86] However, of all the efforts made in behalf of the Indians none surpassed the return of land to Indian communities and the settlement of land disputes in their favor.[87] The Carrera decades witnessed increasing agrarian diversification and an escape from the monoculture which had characterized agriculture for so long. In sum, the conditions for the Indian majority improved during the Carrera years.[88]

While some studies have concentrated recently on the administration and programs of the Carrera administration, scant attention has been given to the philosophical views of Carrera and of his government concerning the Indians and the many complex problems of a dual society. As has been stated, the government realized that its strength rested upon Indian support and certainly exerted efforts to protect and help the Indians, but the impression often remains that Carrera acted more from *realpolitik* than from conviction, that he was more paternalistic than egalitarian. Those paternal and pragmatic aspects of governmental policy seem most readily evident, and this should not be surprising, since Guatemalans had inherited centuries of Spanish paternalism. Furthermore, the anthropological thought emanating from Europe in the nineteenth century ranked the Indian as inferior, and it is assumed that at their most benevolent the Latin American governments exercised an appropriate paternalism toward the native inhabitants but withheld any recognition of real equality. Indeed, the policies of most governments confronting the Indian populations were to insist on their absorption into the Europeanizing patterns, or eradication. The Carrera government offered a refreshing deviation. Despite the intellectual climate in which Carrera governed, there exists some reason to speculate that certain policy makers, among them the president, maintained an unusually open and enlightened attitude toward the Indians, rare anywhere in the nineteenth century and a harbinger of ideas which would take another century to germinate. The evidence is still spotty and begs further research. These suggestions are based on scattered—but neglected—evidence. First and foremost are the actions of the government, which, unlike so many later governments in Latin America, acted for the benefit of the Indians and to a large extent in conformity with Indian demands. But there were also some philosophical pronouncements scattered throughout the Carrera years which provide a glimpse of official thinking.

Carrera's *Informe* to the legislature in 1848 remains one of his major policy statements. In it, he criticized the elites' abuses of the Indians, displayed a laudable understanding of Indian psychology, and expressed his concern for and sympathy with the Indian peoples, who, he emphasized, composed "two-thirds of the Republic's population." In his view, "humanity" and "common sense" required a fair treatment of that majority, which would be best served by the old laws and practices to which they were accustomed.[89] Similar views were discussed on other occasions to reveal, on the one hand, that official philosophy did not change through the years, but, on the other hand, that it was difficult to overcome prejudices apparently ingrained in the Europeanized segment of the population. In 1862 *El Noticioso* carried a significant essay entitled "El antagonismo de razas," which expressed the official attitude in the later years of the Carrera period. While succumbing to the conclusion that European civilization was "superior" and thus subscribing to the racial implications of that conclusion, the essay warned that to accept the Anglo-Saxon version of European civilization would condemn the Indians to extermination, a condition unacceptable to the essay's author. The solution seemed to be the introduction of European civilization as filtered through the more acceptable Spanish experience; within the framework of Spanish Europe and Indian America, Guatemala could forge its own civilization.[90]

Within a month, *El Noticioso* returned to that theme in a clever essay, "Fantasía," signed by Miguel Boada y Balmes. The author called for nothing less than equal rights for the Indians, a singular demand in a hemisphere which at that time adamantly denied everything to the original inhabitants: ". . . the ideal of the present is the moral, and to a certain point physical, emancipation of the Indians, his freedom to enjoy the right universally admitted to be human. . . ." The author based his arguments on the philosophical views favoring the equality of all men, on Christianity, on social justice, and on the brute economic reality that the Indians produced the wealth others enjoyed.[91] What marks the Carrera experience as unique in Indo-America is the respect the government extended to Indian cultures and the reluctance to push the Indian population into Europeanizing.

A willingness to respect Indian customs did not eliminate the government's attention to "progress." In the relative calm of the last decade and a half of the Carrera government, the dual society both preserved the past and flirted with the future. During the closing years of the period, the newspapers commented frequently on the satisfactory pace of "progress" and "advancement," not hesitating to applaud the maturing "civilization" of Guatemala.[92] President Carrera himself once had reminded the legislature that when he entered office his enemies expected "barbarism" to envelop the country, but that he consistently had fostered "culture and civilization."[93] In the last decade of the century, the novelist Manuel Cabral, writing under the pseudonym of Felipe de Jesús, provided unique insight into Guatemala City during the final Carrera years. The author repeatedly reminisced in his novel *María: Historia de una mártir* that those were happy years for the republic. He made the comparison between his and those times in the following terms:

The beautiful capital of the Republic was around 1860 . . . one of the most tranquil and consequently placidly enchanting cities of Spanish America. Foreigners had not yet taken possession of it and therefore had not introduced those European customs which—let me say it frankly—if they have brought us some advantages have caused us on the other hand much trouble. . . . No, let's not completely forsake the past. Perhaps we find many improvements in our present style of living but at the same time we miss many things which we have lost and whose loss now grieves us. We accept, as we will always accept, with pleasure everything which represents a positive advancement, but at the same time we energetically reject everything which tends to diminish the happiness of the people. Peace of mind, tranquility in the home, purity of customs, public morality are advantages a thousand times more precious than all the inventions and discoveries of modern science. . . . A frenzy for business and with it questionable speculations had not yet invaded us in those bygone days; there was no luxury but there was decency; commerce was limited but more honorable . . . and consequently if misery did exist it was on a very small scale. National industries flourished and prospered even if at a modest rhythm. Today all that has disappeared almost completely because of the importation of European goods. What we once produced ourselves we now import. True, it might be more attractive but it doesn't last as long and is therefore more costly. . . . From such exploitation, from such abuse of our hospitality, our poverty has arisen. What does it matter if today there is greater happiness in certain circles if on the other hand the tears flow more abundantly in the suburbs of our beautiful capital? . . . In those days the number of poor families was few; today they are the majority.[94]

In the fascinating if overly romanticized plot, María, at one time a member of a small, rising middle class, identifies with the Indian past. María confides to her family's former maid, an Indian, "I know that you and alongside of you all the humble daughters of the people, to whose class I belong with all my heart from this day forward, are more generous, better, more unselfish, and nobler than many of those proud aristocrats who believe themselves degraded if they deign to speak a word to us."[95] The novel is significant for many reasons, not the least of which is the nostalgic glance at the Carrera years as representative of a benign period in Guatemalan history when the majority probably lived better than at any other period in the century.

The Indian victory under Carrera proved to be as transitory as the gaucho's under Rosas. The death of Carrera in 1865 reinvigorated the elite's effort to wield power, and they succeeded under the leadership of another and different type of caudillo, Justo Rufino Barrios, 1873–1885. Positivist in orientation, President Barrios duly emphasized order and material progress. Under the Liberal reforms of the post-1871 period, capitalism made its definitive entry into Guatemala, which meant large-scale exportation of coffee with all the attendant consequences for that agrarian economy. The government rushed to import foreign technicians, ideas, and manufactured goods. It did not hesitate to contract foreign loans to pay for the Europeanization. The improvement of roads from the highland plantations to the ports and then the construction of the much desired railroads first to the Pacific and later to the Atlantic accelerated coffee production and integrated Guatemala into the world market system more tightly than ever. As elsewhere, the new railroads were owned and operated by foreigners and paid handsome profits to overseas investors. The burden of financing the railroads as well as the other accouterments of progress inevitably fell on the poor.[96]

Spiraling coffee production for export had several long-range negative consequences. For one thing, it diminished the amount of land, labor, and capital available to produce food for local consumption. Wheat harvests especially declined. Monoculture again became a dominant characteristic of the economy. To create the necessary work force on the coffee *fincas*, the Indians were forced, under a burdensome system of *mandamientos*, to become wage laborers. Meanwhile the government did not hesitate to concede to private landowners many lands on which the Indians had lived and worked for generations but to which they possessed no title under Guatemalan laws more attuned to European than to local experiences. Those laws regarded land without titles as "vacant," and the prospering elite eagerly acquired the acreage.[97] By a variety of means the large estates encroached on the Indians' communal lands. As a consequence the economic and social position of the Indian majority declined.[98] Anthropologists have recorded the negative effect of the coffee plantations on the indigenous cultures, which have never recovered from the shock.[99] The pitiful conditions of the Indians prompted Francisco Lainfiesta, a minister in the Barrios government, to mount an eloquent defense of them in his novel *A vista de pájaro* (1879). Later, in his novel *Edmundo* (1896), José A. Beteta lamented the degradation of the "miserable Indians bent beneath the weight of their rude work. . . . who seemed to cry over the loss of the adored land which belonged to their grandfathers and to sigh for the liberty robbed from them."[100]

The judgments of the Barrios period and the Liberal reforms inevitably point to the material changes, the prosperity of the elites, and the transformation of Guatemala City into a pseudo-European capital. Balancing those accomplishments were a return to monoculture, declining food production for local consumption, rising foreign debt, forced labor, debt peonage, the growth of the latifundia, and the greater impoverishment of the majority. Reflecting once again the common historiographical bias, library shelves groan under the biographical studies of the two nineteenth-century "modernizers," Gálvez and Barrios, while historians continue to ignore Rafael Carrera.

The Indians of Mexico provided other notable examples of grass-roots rebellion. The Yaquis of Sonora fought bitterly against the central government throughout the nineteenth century. The impact of railroad construction and hacienda expansion in Sonora during the Porfiriato intensified their resistance. The new economic enterprises absorbed the Yaquis' land and demanded their labor, forcing them to acquiesce or to fight. José María Leyva Cajeme organized and governed a Yaqui state-within-a-state from 1875 until his death in 1886. Resistance declined before the overwhelming federal forces, but a handful of rebels under Juan Maldonado, alias Tatabiate, raided haciendas, ranches, and mines during the last decade of the century. The government responded to Yaqui rebellion by selling the Indians into virtual slavery to the owners of the labor-short henequen plantations in distant Yucatan.[101]

The Tzotzil Maya of Chiapas rebelled, 1867–1870, under the leadership of Pedro Díaz Cuscat to restore Indian power to the Chiapan highlands and thus rescue the community from Ladino oppression. As one means of creating a new Indian society and religion and of eradicating Ladino influence, the Indians sought to create their own Mayan Christ. To do so, they crucified a ten-year-old Indian boy, who was to become a "new, Indian son of God and Sun/Christ."[102] Bitter ethnic conflict characterized Cuscat's war. Several times the Mayas nearly toppled the state government in San Cristóbal de las Casas before federal and state troops defeated them. Throughout nineteenth-century Mexico, Indian disturbances, which seemed to cluster around the years 1832–1833, 1842–1845, 1849, 1856–1857, 1868–1869, 1878–1882, 1886, 1896, 1906, and 1910, threatened various mestizo communities. The Indians' desire to reassert control over lands they felt traditionally belonged to them sparked most of the uprisings.[103]

Doubtless the major Indian rebellion in terms of length, carnage, and significance was the Caste War of Yucatan between the Mayas and the peninsula's whites and mestizos. In the years after Mexico declared its independence, the sugar and henequen plantations had expanded to threaten the corn culture of the Mayas by incorporating their lands into the latifundia and by impressing the Indians into service as debt peons. The Indians fought for their land and freedom. They defended their world. On the other side, the Yucatan elite professed that they fought for "the holy cause of order, humanity and civilization."[104] Much of the bloodiest fighting occurred during the period 1847–1855, but the war lingered on until the early twentieth century. During those decades the Mayas of eastern and southern Yucatan governed themselves.

Free of white domination, the Mayan rebels took the name of Cruzob, turned their backs on the white world, and developed their own culture, a synthesis of their Mayan inheritance and Spanish influences. Four hundred years of conquest had erased the intellectual and artistic heritage from the Mayan mind, but the Cruzob retained their knowledge of agriculture and village and family organization from the pre-Columbian past. Unique to the Cruzob was the development of their own religion, based largely on their interpretation of Christianity. Unlike other syncretic religions of Latin America, it developed without dependence on the sporadic participation of Roman Catholic priests (to perform baptisms, marriages, or an occasional Mass) and free from the critical eye of the white master. Incorporating the Indian folkways, religion strengthened the Cruzob and provided a spiritual base for independence that other Indians lacked. What was notable about the Cruzob was the emergence of a viable Indian alternative to Europeanization. Although infused with Spanish contributions, it bore a strong resemblance to the pre-Columbian Mayan society.[105] Reviving their Indian culture by repudiating "foreign" domination and substituting their own values for "foreign" ones, the Cruzob revitalized their society. They became masters in their own land again.[106]

Powerful forces at work in the closing decades of the nineteenth century overwhelmed the Cruzob. The poor soil of Yucatan, exhausted under corn cultivation, no longer yielded sufficient food. Disease reduced the Indian ranks faster than battle did. At the same time, the increasingly stable Mexico under Porfirio Díaz showed less tolerance for the Cruzob and more determination to subdue them in order to exploit Yucatan. A treaty between Mexico and Great Britain closed British

Honduras to the Cruzob, thus cutting off their single source of modern weapons and ammunition. Finally, the expanding railroads and roads from northern Yucatan accompanying the prosperous henequen plantations penetrated the Cruzob territory. A growing market for forest woods sent the whites even into the seemingly impenetrable forest redoubts of the Cruzob. Consequently a declining Cruzob population and relentless Mexican pressures brought to an end the Mayan independence of half a century. The long and tenacious Indian resistance testified to the Indian preferences, a rejection of the Europeanization preferred by the elites.

In Ecuador, Indian uprisings punctuated the nineteenth century. Oswaldo Albornoz P. has chronicled twenty such rebellions caused by increased taxation, harsh exploitation, and a desire to defend or recover communal lands.[107] One of the major rebellions broke out in 1871 in Chimborazo province, where the Indians sought to end the abuses and crushing taxation of the Gabriel García Moreno government. The chief of the rebellion, Francisco Daquidema, was condemned to death by a military tribunal and has been banished from "history" by Ecuadorian historians. Peruvian history witnessed similar Indian protest. Overwork, excessive taxation, and general abuse goaded the Indians to rebel in Puno in 1866 and in Ancash in 1885. In the latter uprising the Indians captured the departmental capital, Huaráz, and several other towns before the army dispersed them. The Indian leader Pedro Pablo Atusparia emerged from the struggle as a genuine folk hero revered by his people, although—to repeat a well-established pattern by now—ignored by the official histories of Peru. Still, three remarkable intellectuals, Juan Bustamente, Clorinda Matto de Turner, and Manuel González Prada, attempted to focus national attention on the plight of the indigenous population. The first was executed; the second sent into exile.

In those nations where slavery lingered after independence, the blacks vigorously protested their servitude and the institutions which allowed it. They threatened the local slaveholders and intensified the anxieties of the governments. Visions of the successful slave revolt in Haiti haunted the elites. Unrelenting black pressure through guerrilla warfare finally persuaded the Colombian government to free the remaining slaves in 1852. Major slave threats to established order occurred in Venezuela in 1835 and Peru in 1848. Brazilian slaves constantly rebelled until final abolition in 1888. In fact, the period just prior to abolition, 1882–1887, witnessed a sharp increase in rebellions, runaways, and assassinations of slaveowners.[108] Perhaps the major slave revolt occurred in 1835 in Bahia, scene of nine revolts or attempts since the opening of the century. Well organized and directed by Nagos slaves, the rebels sought to kill all whites and to free all slaves. Though the uprising failed, it sent shivers of fear throughout the white community which never abated until slavery was abolished. Sober members of the elites regarded the slave as "a volcano that constantly threatens society, a mine ready to explode," as Agostinho Marques Perdigao Malheiros phrased it in his authoritative study *A escravidão no Brasil* (1866). Foreign visitors sensed the tension. The European Prince Adalbert visited one large and well-run plantation which he praised as a model. After noting the seemingly friendly relations between the master and the slaves, he revealed, "The loaded guns and pistols hanging up in his [the master's] bedroom however, showed that he had not entire confidence in them [the slaves] and indeed, he had more than once been obliged to face them with his loaded gun."[109] The story of the slave rebellions and of the reactions of the Latin American blacks to their society in the nineteenth century remains to be told. Although historians take note of some of the blacks' protests against the nineteenth century's most brutal institution, they inevitably credit abolition to one or another enlightened "Europeanized" president or leader, treating it as a gift generously bestowed on grateful blacks, failing to do justice to the struggle of a determined people to win its own freedom.[110]

Novelists, although often sympathetic in their prose to the plight of the blacks, generally failed to depict the reality of being a slave—or, for that matter, a black—in a Europeanized society, but they did suggest the status of racial relations and a degree of societal violence. In her novel *Sab* (1841), the Cuban Gertrudis Gómez de Avellaneda made the faithful mulatto slave Sab sacrifice the wealth acquired from a winning lottery ticket for his master's family, a symbolic gesture revealing the whites' perception of the blacks' role. To further carry out the symbolism, Carlota, daughter of Sab's master and object of the black's affections, to whom he secretly transfers the lottery ticket, marries an English merchant, and, although she may not be happy, she travels widely, lives well, and apparently fulfills the island's desire of union with the new metropolis. Later in the century, Aluizio Azevedo related in *O mulato* (1881) how Raimundo felt as a light-skinned, blue-eyed mulatto in Brazilian society, in an exposé of the subtleties of racial prejudice.[111] Sab, the slave, commits suicide, forced to self-destruction by society; Raimundo, the free mulatto, is assassinated, a vengeance society wreaks upon him because he dares to be the equal of the "white" Brazilians. These novelists were recording the reality that, free or slave, the person of African descent was caught in the maelstrom of violence in nineteenth-century Latin America.

Other popular segments of the varied Latin American populations had joined the rebellion against accelerating Europeanization. The Brazilian provinces shook with protest. Bahia, in particular, during the years 1824–1840, had seethed with social tension. In general terms it is safe to conclude that the Bahian rebels were people of color who opposed or fought against the "European types." Their ideology was vague and often contradictory. They frequently sacked shops and warehouses in a quest for food and killed military officers and landowners in a challenge to authority.[112]

In the 1830s, also, three major popular rebellions had revealed the unrest in the northeast and north of Brazil: the War of the Cabanos in the interior of Pernambuco and Alagoas, 1832–1836; the Cabanagem in Pará, 1835–1840; and the Balaiada in Maranhão, 1838–1841. These three, of the many which rocked the empire in that turbulent decade, appear to have had the most popular support and expressed the frustrations of poor whites, mestizos, mulattoes, black slaves, and Indians. The rebels hoped to improve their standards of living, although their programs were vague, and to share in the exercise of power. The War of the Cabanos was particularly significant because it was entirely rural-based. The leader, Vicente Ferreira da Paula, is considered to be an "authentic leader of the masses," according to a revisionist study of the rebellion.[113] The leaders of the three rebellions were revered by their followers, who considered each of them to be one of themselves; however, to the governments, they were "criminals," "bandits," and "outlaws," as they are still termed whenever mentioned in the official histories. For example, in a history text widely used during the 1960s in Brazilian universities, the author spoke of the Balaiada as "unchecked banditry," and the principal allegation against the rebels is their "audacity to attack private property."[114] The proclamation in 1840 that the young Pedro II was of age to reign and his subsequent coronation strengthened the control of the elites but did not eliminate displays of popular wrath and contradiction. The Ronco da Abeha revolt in Paraiba in 1852 and the Movimento dos Marimbondos in Pernambuco at the same time objected to the new law requiring civil registration of birth, a requirement suspected by the people of color as a means to enslave them. As often happened in Latin America, these people saw in the Roman Catholic Church a protector, while they suspected the State of being the exploiter. As a result of the uprisings, Church registration continued until 1889, after the abolition of slavery. Other popular manifestations disturbed the order dear to the Brazilian elite: the Carne sem Osso movement in 1858 and the Vintem in 1880.

The Quebra-Quilo Revolt, late 1874 to early 1875, ranked high in significance because the peasants of the interior of the Northeast succeeded in checking the Brazilian government's new modernization drive, under way by 1871 but ineffectual by 1875. The causes of the revolt were not unique: new taxes and the peasants' fear that the large landowners were absorbing their farms, complicated by the imposition of the metric system and the required payment of fees for official conversion and authentication of weights. A journalist covering the revolt attributed it to "the direct consequence of the suffering and deprivation . . . [of] the working classes of the interior," while a peasant participant claimed, "The fruit of the soil belongs to the people and tax ought not be paid on it."[115] As riots multiplied in the marketplaces from Rio Grande do Norte to Alagoas, the municipal and provincial authorities feared that the "forces of Barbarism" were poised to sweep across the Northeast. The peasants were unusually successful. They did not pay the new taxes; they destroyed the new weights and measures; they burned official records and archives, thus protecting their informal title to the land by reducing to ashes the legal records. In most cases, those peasants had taken physical possession of the land and worked it over the generations without title. They faced possible eviction by anyone who could show the proper paper authenticating legal ownership. By destroying records, the peasants removed evidence—the local notarial registers of land, for example—from use in judicial proceedings, thereby putting themselves on equal legal footing with the local landed elite. Momentarily, then, the sporadic riots which constituted the revolt achieved the peasants' goals, while temporarily frustrating the penetration of the elites into their region.[116]

Popular protests were not unique to Brazil. In Argentina, too, the common people expressed their disagreement with elitist rule. In the six years after Buenos Aires took control of the newly centralized government and President Mitre determined to impose urban, elitist government over folk cultures (1862–1868), Argentina witnessed 117 rebellions with ninety-one battles and the death of 4,728 citizens.[117] The forms that modernization assumed in Latin America—the expansion of the latifundia oriented toward export, the construction of railways with the resultant opening to export agriculture of regions once linked with folk societies, the encouragement of European immigration with land grants—ignited protest, rebellion, and uprisings throughout Latin America. Angered by the absorption of their lands by the growing latifundia, armed groups of men circulated through the streets of Cali, Colombia, on the nights of May 20 and 21, 1848, shouting, "Long live the people and death to the whites!" Then they tore down fences erected by two hacendados which had deprived the peasants of pasture for their animals. Governor Vicente Borrero of the province of Buenaventura noted in a letter the following month to President

Tomás Cipriano de Mosquera, "The People are constantly at war with the Landowners, and the Landowners with the People."[118] In a cogent essay connecting railroad construction with the growth of large estates in Mexico, John Coatsworth emphasizes that accelerated railroad building between 1877 and 1884 encouraged the proliferation and expansion of latifundias near the tracks, and this in turn aroused the Indian communities to rebellion, a reaction to their loss of land.[119] Revolts shook the province of Santa Fe in Argentina in 1893, triggered on the one hand by small farmers' protests against a tax on wheat to pay for the government's innovations, including railroads, and on the other by the resentment of the *criollos* because immigrants received land and preferred treatment denied the locals.[120] Thus the pace of modernization partly accounts for the rebellion and its attendant violence in nineteenth-century Latin America.

Popular protest assumed forms other than rebellion. Banditry and millenarian movements flourished in the nineteenth century, although serious studies of them are still extremely rare. Thanks to the conceptual framework offered by E. J. Hobsbawm, it is possible to consider banditry as a form of social protest and millenarianism as a type of popular revolution.[121] It now remains for historians to identify the bandits and the millenarian movements as a first step toward understanding their significance in nineteenth-century Latin America. Brazil seems to offer numerous examples of both in the past century. Intensifying urbanization, the growth of commercial agriculture, and the expansion of transportation and communication challenged the folkways of the rural population and sparked cultural conflicts. The despair of the rural masses, their rejection of the present, and their longing for a better life in the future, in turn, gave rise to millenarian movements.[122]

In the backlands of Pernambuco, 1817–1820, Silvestre José dos Santos established the City of Heaven on Earth, where his followers expected riches during their temporal life to be distributed by the mystic sixteenth-century Portuguese monarch Sebastian, the perennial hope of the dispossessed. In 1836–1839, miserably poor people concentrated in Pedra Bonita in the arid interior of Pernambuco to await the metamorphosis of the barren rocks into an enchanted city in which they would enjoy grace, riches, and power, once again through the intervention of King Sebastian. As previously mentioned, in Canudos in 1893–1897, Antônio Conselheiro attracted throngs of faithful followers, discouraged with contemporary Brazil and hopeful of improvement. In the extreme south of Brazil, a messianic movement among German immigrants occurred between 1872 and 1898. Jacobina Maurer, the self-proclaimed reincarnation of Jesus Christ, announced the end of the world and life everlasting for her followers. Parenthetically, this movement offers one of the very few examples of female leadership during the nineteenth century. Periodically throughout the century, small messianic movements flourished in the Amazon basin. In the tribes deculturated by missionaries and explorers, the Indians developed a syncretic religion, part Roman Catholic, part that of their ancestors. They turned to that religion for unity and hope. The messianic movements which appeared denounced "white civilization" as the source of local misery and announced a new and perfect life in which the whites would not be present.[123] These millenarian movements revealed both the spiritual and the temporal needs of the people who subscribed to them, a denunciation of the society in which they dwelled, and a longing for a better life.[124] Similar to the folk cultures already discussed, the millenarian movements evinced a strict hierarchy of authority in which the acknowledged leader ruled supremely and—it was assumed—always in the best interests of the people.

Banditry attracted the desperate, those who had lost out in the system, whether they were the poor or members of the impoverished gentry. Whatever else banditry may have included or meant, it was as much a means of protesting an injustice or righting a wrong as it was of equalizing the wealth or taking political revenge.[125] To the rich and powerful, bandits were outlaws meriting severe punishment; to the poor masses, however, they sometimes represented justice and liberation.[126] Bandits roamed the Brazilian interior in the nineteenth century, particularly in the impoverished Northeast, where many won the admiration of the poor and the respect of the wealthy, who not infrequently co-opted them and utilized their services. Brazilian popular poetry abounds with tales of the bandit hero. A well known poem sung at the beginning of the twentieth century, related the story of Antonio Silvino, who became a *Cangaceiro* in 1896 to avenge an injustice: the slaying of his father by a police official who went unpunished by the government.[127]

Banditry characterized much of Spanish Latin America as well. Peru offers numerous examples of peasant bandits.[128] In his study of Peruvian banditry, Enrique López Albujar described it as "a protest, a rebellion, a deviation, or a simple means of subsistence."[129] He concluded that nineteenth-century Peruvian banditry produced folk heroes like Palomo, Pajarito, Sambambé, and Luis Pardo because those bandits corrected injustices, robbed to help the poor, and protested social and economic inequities—social objectives Albujar did not find prevalent in twentieth-century banditry.[130] Bandits flourish in Spanish American literature, populating the pages of novels and short stories written both in the last century and in the present. Ignacio Manuel Altamirano provided a critical but sympathetic account of the protagonist in *El Zarco* (written in 1888 but published in 1901 and later translated into English as *El Zarco, the Bandit*). Eloping with El Zarco in the final pages of the novel, the character Manuela accepts a not unusual rationalization for banditry: "That El Zarco and his followers were bandits—men who had made robbery and kidnapping their profession—did not seem particularly strange to her, for political leaders in revolt against the government often used the same methods. To her, the bandits were rebels at war with society, their cruelty a natural reaction to a life of constant danger."[131] Indeed, Altamirano has already informed his readers that El Zarco became a bandit after "tiring of a life of servitude and poverty."[132] In short, banditry became a means of protest against social and economic injustice. Similarly in an early Guatemalan novella, D. Bouquet y Soler took an understanding and sympathetic view of a bandit. Falling into the hands of Monreal, widely feared as the most infamous bandit of Central America, the narrator finds him to be "courteous and decent," an intelligent individual. Significantly, in this story, Monreal reveals to the narrator the glories of Guatemala's Indian past by taking him to a lost Mayan city.[133] The literary bandits incarnated idealizations of one sort or another, the recognition by one group of intellectuals of just causes for dissatisfaction among the masses. In ascribing a nobility to the bandits, these writers implied a need for social reforms. The real bandits probably revealed a character more harmonious with desperation. Their motives and activities varied widely, but at least in part they could be explained as protests against the wrongs of society as the bandits viewed it. Because of their strength and because they often opposed the elites and official institutions, they received the support, indeed, the admiration of large numbers of the humble classes, who often hid them, lied to the authorities to protect them, guided them through strange terrain, and fed them. To the poor, they were caudillos who by default helped to sustain the folk cultures.

Of the varied alternatives offered to the Europeanization imposed by the urban elites, few at this point in research seem clear in either their goals or their methods. Most were protests, expressions of dissatisfaction with urban growth, exotic ideas and customs, foreign presence, higher taxes, forced labor, vaccination, loss of land, and affronts to local traditions. Much basic research will be required before authoritative conclusions can be drawn from nineteenth-century popular protest.[134] For the present, one can only speculate that larger numbers of Latin Americans, probably the majority, seemed to prefer their folk cultures. Some of the rural elites concurred with popular sentiments, but their reasoning may have included a reluctance to disturb their comfortable position as much as a loyalty to the past. The popular rebellions, protests, banditry, and millenarianism, albeit diverse in their Latin American manifestations over the course of a century, had their roots in folk culture. Those preferences by no means rejected change in order to preserve the past unaltered. Rather, the folk cultures would mediate change over a longer period of time. The folk—and a portion of the elites—refused to denounce their Ibero-Afro-Indian heritage in order to import wholesale ideas, artifacts, and life-styles of Northern Europe and the United States. The Indians, not surprisingly, looked to their own rich past with its well-defined customs, languages, and relationships; still, they recognized the input of the conquerors' innovations. The Cruzob, for example, embraced cultural patterns which did not replicate those of their Mayan forebears but rather demonstrated a pragmatic blend of cultures confected by centuries of exposure to European institutions. Vague as the concept of "inorganic democracy" might appear in retrospect, it did hold meaning to the gauchos who identified it with their life-style, a unique adaptation of limited aspects of European civilization to the demands of the pampas. The gauchos' success in their environment was their best resistance for a long time to a determined Europeanization of Argentina fostered by the elites of Buenos Aires. The very persistence of folk cultures testifies to the satisfactory life-style they offered millions of Latin Americans.

Doubtless the most successful resistance to Europeanization took place in Paraguay, where, during the decades from 1810 to 1870, a native alternative took form, influenced in almost equal parts by the American and the European past.[135] Since Paraguay challenged the trend to Europeanize more effectively than any other group or nation, it merits, as a form of conclusion, special attention. Three caudillos dominated Paraguay in the 1810–1870 period: José Gaspar Rodríguez de Francia (1814–1840), Antonio Carlos López (1840–1863), and Francisco Solano López (1863–1870). Francia charted the course for Paraguay's autonomous revolution, which insured economic independence and possibly the only example of economic development in nineteenth-century Latin America. With only minimal contacts with the outside world, the landlocked nation under Francia's leadership emerged as the most egalitarian society yet known in the Western Hemisphere. He accomplished this unique development by eliminating from power several mighty groups whose governments in the rest of Latin America perpetuated the area's economic dependency. Francia nationalized the Roman Catholic Church, confiscating its temporal goods, abolishing the tithe, and decreeing religious freedom. Thus he not only eliminated a potential rival but avoided the Church-State conflicts which eroded national harmony throughout most of Latin America. He removed the traditional, although small and modest, elites from power and destroyed their base of prestige and wealth by nationalizing most of their estates. In possession of the majority of the nation's land, the government established scores of prosperous state ranches and rented the rest for a nominal fee to anyone willing to till the soil. No latifundia dominated the economy, nor did monocultural export deform it. Paraguay became self-sufficient in the production of food. While the establishment of a state iron works and state textile and livestock industries provided employment for thousands of Paraguayans, small handicraft industries further augmented national production, thereby meeting the simple, basic needs of the people. Through a rigidly enforced system of trade licenses and its own massive participation, the state prevented the growth of a native or foreign commercial class; no foreign interests were permitted to penetrate the economy; nor did foreign debts, loans, or interest rates hobble it. Francia regulated commerce and controlled the economy to achieve national goals rather than to permit a small group to satisfy individual desires. New information indicates that a rudimentary educational system, satisfactory for the needs of a simple agrarian society, practically eliminated illiteracy.

Continuing on that autonomous course in the three decades after Francia's death, the two Lópezes, father and son, saw to it that Paraguay not only built a railroad, strung telegraph lines, and constructed its own modern steamship navy to ply its abundant waterways, but also put into operation Latin America's first iron foundry. The two caudillos achieved these innovations without incurring foreign debt and for the benefit of the Paraguayans. Thereby, Paraguay continued to enjoy economic as well as political independence, escaping the neo-colonial dependency characteristic of nineteenth-century Latin America.

The rapid and genuine development of Paraguay under its own form of "inorganic democracy" alarmed the elitist governments in neighboring states whose own export-oriented economies had grown but failed to develop. They accused

Paraguay of upsetting the balance of power in the Río de la Plata. More realistically, they feared the appealing example Paraguay offered to wider segments of their own populations. Argentina, Brazil, and their puppet-state Uruguay joined forces in the War of the Triple Alliance to bring "civilization" to "barbarian" Paraguay (1864–1870). The Paraguayan masses proved their devotion to their caudillo by fighting tenaciously against their huge neighbors and keeping at bay armies many times their size for over five years. Financed in part by English loans, the allies waged a war of genocide, killing approximately 90 percent of Paraguay's adult male population. During the five years of occupation following the war, the allies dismantled the popular institutions of Paraguay's autonomous revolution. They opened the nation to foreign capital and attendant debt. The land passed from the hands of the state and the peasants into huge unused or underused estates typical of the land patterns of the rest of Latin America. Paraguay's alternative to Europeanization was ended forcibly in 1870, and thereafter the standard mold of nineteenth-century Latin American institutions characterized that nation.

The Paraguayan experiment is of considerable interest in the study of nineteenth-century Latin America. It existed long enough, more than half a century, to offer a viable alternative to Europeanization with its cosmetic modernization and pervasive and deepening dependency. Paraguay provides the best example of what might have occurred had local traditions and preferences won in the intense cultural clash which convulsed Latin America. It offered an example of folk society absorbing and implementing selected aspects of European technology for the benefit of the folk. Thus it represented an alternative to the dichotomy of either folk society or Europeanization.

## Modernization and Impoverishment

Modernization triumphed over the folk cultures. By the end of the nineteenth century the Latin American nations had acquired many of the accouterments of progress. Railroads expanded, the ports boasted the newest equipment, telegraph and telephone wires hummed. An incipient industrialization was under way and the cities were on the threshold of a major population explosion. Intellectual, cultural, financial, commercial, and social links with Europe and the United States were strengthened. Many people celebrated the apparent transformation of Latin America and hailed the evident progress as desirable. Certainly, benefits accrued to some Latin Americans, but that coin of prosperity also revealed another side.

Progress did not alter the fundamental institutions inherited from the colonial past. Ironically, it strengthened the negative aspects of some fundamental ones such as the latifundia with its monoculture, labor exploitation, and socioeconomic privileges for the landowner to the detriment of the rural masses. Real or meaningful modernization was impossible to achieve because the elites refused to reform the inherited colonial institutions. The cosmetic effects of modernization satisfied them, just as the consequences of thoroughly implementing their goal frightened them. This is understandable: they profited from their relationship with the metropolis. In fact, the elites enjoyed the best of two worlds: the superficial modernization enhanced their immediate comforts and flattered their image of themselves, while at the same time it permitted them to blame the "barbaric" masses for delaying or frustrating further modernization.

Unmistakably, the dependency of all of Latin America deepened as modernization accelerated. Thus the implementation of the modernization, either chosen by the Latin American elites or imposed by outside capital investment, actually debilitated Latin America. The new railroads, ports, steamships, technical aid, and loans tied and subordinated the Latin American economy to England and the United States and to a lesser degree to France and Germany. In a comparison of the relations of Great Britain with Uruguay and New Zealand in the nineteenth century, Robin W. Winks has concluded that the South American nation was as much a colony of the British as New Zealand was.[136]

Chile offers one example of how modernization could

contribute to change a relatively balanced export economy into one more dependent on the exportation of a single natural product. Throughout the first three-quarters of the nineteenth century, Chile exported both agricultural goods and minerals. In the 1845–1850 period, agriculture accounted for 45 percent of total exports, while silver, gold, and copper accounted for most of the rest. By the opening of the decade of the 1880s that balance had disappeared. Due to the upsurge in nitrate production, mining represented 78 percent of the exports in 1881. Thereafter, Chile depended heavily on the export of one mineral, first nitrates and then copper, for its export earnings. The building of railroads, the improvement of other forms of transportation, the renovation of ports, the importation of machinery and technology, the invitations to foreign experts, the increase in foreign investment, all encouraged modernization but also contributed to the concentration on mineral exports.[137]

Costa Rica provides a most sobering example of how modernization allowed foreigners to take control of a national economy. To market larger quantities of coffee and thus earn the money to modernize, during the period 1870–1890 the government encouraged the construction of a railroad from the highlands where the coffee grew to Puerto Limón for shipment abroad. The onerous loans overburdened the treasury as the government paid usurious interest rates to unscrupulous foreign money-lenders. Further, the government bestowed on Minor Keith, the chief engineer, 800,000 acres, land which fronted on the railroad and later became the center of the plantations of the United Fruit Company. Even so, the railroad remained in foreign hands. British investors also controlled the ports, mines, electric lighting, major public works, and foreign commerce as well as the principal domestic marketplaces. In short, Costa Rica surrendered all its economic independence and mortgaged its future in order to attain the accouterments of modernization. No evidence exists that any Costa Ricans except a tiny elite benefited.[138]

The extent to which economic development resulted from the elitist policies that characterized nineteenth-century Latin America requires clarification. *Development* is the utilization of a nation's potential for the greatest benefit of the largest number of the inhabitants, and must be contrasted with *growth*, which denotes simply numerical accumulation, and with the type of *modernization* the Latin Americans imported. More often than not, the elites willfully or innocently confused development with growth or modernization, a not uncommon confusion which still characterizes studies of Latin America. Growth occurred, although it was sporadic and cyclical.[139] Modernization took place, too, but of a type more useful to the metropolis than to Latin America. Scant evidence of development exists. The elites' devotion to Europe in the last analysis subjected Latin America's well-being to that of their distant mentor and fostered an economic dependency which entailed political subordination, cultural imitation, and social inequity. Because the elites contrived or adopted the national policies, whatever the outside pressures, and enforced those policies, however erratically or imperfectly, they bear much of the responsibility for mortgaging Latin America's future and perpetuating or increasing the poverty of the majority.

With diminishing access to land and accelerating commercialization of agriculture, the rural masses were victims of contracting economic options. Their wages stagnated or declined. Nutritional standards deteriorated. In short, the quality of life for the majority fell.[140]

Perhaps the most thorough documentation of the declining quality of life exists for rural Mexico. In 1810, total corn production averaged two pounds per Mexican per day; by 1919 it had fallen to less than one pound.[141] It has been estimated that real wages in 1910 were but one-quarter of those of 1810.[142] Nineteenth-century commentators on the life-style of the rural Indian masses often observed that it was worse than during the colonial period. In 1834, *La Palabra* noted, "The Indians today find themselves in a worse situation than under the vice-royalty," an observation repeated in 1887 by *El Libre y Aceptado Masón*: "For them [the Indians], we are worse than the conquerors. The Indians are the docile instruments of the reactionaries, and if they look to the past it is because their present situation is worse than the old one."[143] The misery of Mexico's Indian and mestizo masses increased to dismal proportions during the three and a half decades of the Díaz government, when their buying power slipped rapidly.[144] Bean and corn per capita production fell; corn prices rose.[145] The rural laborers were eating less of the basic agricultural crops in 1910 than they had in 1877.[146]

During the last half, and particularly the last quarter, of the nineteenth century, the quality of life of the Argentine rural masses sharply declined. The export boom benefited the large landowner but bypassed entire regions and whole social classes. Real wages of the rural workers declined.[147] Carl Solberg has concluded that between 1884 and 1899 real wages fell a full 20 percent.[148] In the province of Tucumán, the newspaper *La Razón* pointed out on several occasions in the 1880s that Brazilian slaves lived better than the local peons did. The sugar boom of that province in no way alleviated the misery and debt peonage which became increasingly characteristic of the working class there.[149] For Guatemala, David J. McCreery has indicated the negative effects of coffee exports and national legislation on the Indians' standard of living during the last quarter of the century.[150] In a seminal study of Chilean rural labor, Arnold J. Bauer has noted that rising export demands made on the haciendas after mid-century caused deterioration of the quality of life among the workers. The old system of *inquilinaje* became more demanding, imposing a heavier work load on rural labor while at the same time the *inquilinos* received smaller land allotments.[151] By the last decade of the century, real wages for the Chilean rural workers "most likely" were falling.[152]

For Brazil, the coffee boom of the last half of the century brought prosperity to a limited region of that vast subcontinent. There, per capita income increased; but those figures can be misleading. Nathaniel H. Leff warns us, "While the income of domestic landowners was increasing, the elastic supply of labor had a dampening effect on upward wage movements. Under these conditions, the growth in incomes consequent upon export expansion probably led to an increase in the inequality of income distribution within the expanding export region."[153] Whatever prosperity characterized the cof-

fee boom in the Southeast had to be weighed with declines
elsewhere in the economy, particularly in the Northeast,
where the dominant sugar industry was undergoing a series
of prolonged crises. In that region, real wages deteriorated
after 1870 and the rural wage earner suffered a falling standard of living.[154] After an exhaustive study of that sugar industry, Peter L. Eisenberg concludes that "the free rural laborers in the later nineteenth century enjoyed little material
advantage over the slave."[155] William Paul McGreevey, in *An
Economic History of Colombia, 1845–1930*, offers one of the
most damning indictments of the effects of the pseudo-European institutions on the welfare of the majority. He concludes, "Income apparently declined for significant groups of
the Colombian population in the second half of the nineteenth century."[156] From the evidence now at hand, a pre-
liminary conclusion can be drawn that for the rural masses,
deprived of land, offered low salaries whose buying power
diminished over the course of a century, and forced to sub-
sist on an increasingly restricted and less nutritious diet, the
quality of life declined as the century waned.

The above discussion concentrates on the rural sector because an overwhelming majority of the Latin Americans in
the nineteenth century lived in the countryside, and because
more data on their standard of living are available. Probably
the situation for the majority of the urban dwellers was no
better. McGreevey discloses a shift of income in urban Columbia from poor artisans to well-to-do merchants.[157] Real
industrial wages in Mexico amounted to less in 1910 than
they had a generation earlier.[158] James R. Scobie has provided
some valuable if bleak statistics on the rising cost of living
in Buenos Aires, 1870–1910, coupled with some declining
salaries.[159] Concluding that the cost of living for the urban
working class was disproportionately high, Scobie offers these
statistics to illustrate the economic problems the family
faced: "The top monthly wage a day laborer could earn in
1901 amounted to 70 pesos *moneda nacional* (m$n), or the
equivalent of 30 gold pesos. The estimated minimum expenses for an average worker family totaled 100 pesos m$n, or
43 gold pesos."[160] Aldo Ferrer also testifies that prices out-

stripped wages in Argentine cities, allocating to the workers a small share of the income generated by industry.[161] In her studies of wages and prices in Rio de Janeiro, Eulália M. L. Lobo has noted, "A general tendency of lower acquisitive power of salaries manifested itself in the second half of the nineteenth century."[162] Increasingly, other research in other areas of Latin America outlines the same urban pattern.[163]

A stagnant or declining quality of life was only one disadvantage modernization inflicted on the majority. It also subverted their cultural and spiritual values. Modernization as it occurred in nineteenth-century Latin America did not seem to benefit the largest number of the people to the degree that the folk cultures or societies had.

Folk or popular caudillos arose in nineteenth-century Latin America who possessed the ability to mediate folk and European values and under whose leadership the majority seemed to draw some benefits. Carrera, Rosas, and Francia serve as the best examples. Some regional folk societies, Canudos in Brazil or the Cruzob in Yucatan, managed also to provide benefits for the majority. It must be remembered, however, that most local or regional folk leaders remain anonymous, unrecorded by history. From all accounts the people under those folk-oriented governments identified with their policies, enjoyed psychic benefits, and seemingly achieved material well-being. From the available evidence, Paraguay under the folk caudillos seems to be the nation in nineteenth-century Latin America which offers the best example of genuine development as contrasted with growth. Further, that development was accompanied by some modernization. True, the life-style of the rustic Paraguayan population was simple to the extreme. Yet, if recent research is correct the people had access to land, ate a nourishing diet, enjoyed adequate housing and minimal education, and felt the satisfaction of close communal life. In short, the quality of life for the majority was satisfactory or better. There is reason to believe that nowhere else in Latin America over such a long time span did the majority so benefit.

Elsewhere, progress as conceived and implemented by the elites tended not only to impoverish but to deculturate the majority. As the folk cultures lost to modernization, the options for the majority diminished. The varieties of life-styles were more evident and divergent at the opening of the century than at the closing. The contrasting life-styles of the majority under their folk cultures and under the elite-directed and elite-oriented modernization suggest why the majority often protested violently against rapid modernization and why these protests were answered with equal ferocity by the elites, who felt they benefited from modernization. Those struggles marked the last effort of the folk to protect their own cultures. The nineteenth century was a violent century, and the extent of the conflicts still begs further research.

To broaden the view of Latin America's recent past to include the intense cultural conflicts opens a wide range of infrequently mentioned topics, not the least of which would be a discussion of communal life-styles advocated by the majority. Such a view diversifies an otherwise homogeneous history as well as focuses attention on the plurality of solutions to Latin America's problems of development. The study of cultural conflicts provides some insight into the constant enigma of prevalent poverty in a potentially wealthy region. Finally, it offers an interpretation which gives greater meaning to the diverse events in nineteenth-century Latin America. It was not after all, a century of random conflicts, meaningless civil wars, and pervasive chaos, but one in which those who favored modernization struggled with those loyal to their folk cultures. The triumph of modernization set the course for twentieth-century history.

*Thomas E. Skidmore* **Workers and Soldiers: Urban Labor Movements and Elite Responses in Twentieth-Century Latin America**

FOR THREE DECADES much of the study of labor in Latin America by North American and European scholars has been part of the study of labor in "developing" countries.[1] In this approach Latin America is included with the "new" nations of Africa, South Asia, and Southeast Asia, most of which escaped European colonial rule only after 1945. The historical development of these "new" nations has been telescoped, leaving labor organizations with no time to establish their bona fides as authentic and autonomous. Most often they have been subordinated to, sometimes absorbed into, the prevailing independence political movement. As a result, it is difficult, if not impossible to sort out the history of organized labor and analyze its independent role.[2]

Latin America does not fit this mold. Political independence was achieved a century and a half ago. There followed a long period in which economic development and labor organization could take place. Authors such as Millen, Sufrin, Kerr, and Galenson, who wrote and published in the late 1950s and early 1960s, are of little help on Latin America when they attempt to explain the behavior of labor throughout the developing world.[3] Most such approaches are further weakened by reliance on the dated and unsatisfactory concept of "modernization." Because the variables are ill-defined, the factual documentation thin, and the level of generalization high, these surveys do not offer useful analytical approaches.

More helpful for students of Latin American labor history are the research findings in two other areas. One is the study of labor history—broadly conceived—in the U.S. and Europe, where comparative investigation offers important clues for Latin Americanists.[4] We should begin by noting that the writing of European and North American working-class history has been recently challenged by a new approach. A revisionist group has sought to broaden the focus of labor history to include all working people (defined as blue-collar workers), not simply those in unions, as in most traditional historiography. There has also been a call to look at the full range of workers' lives, to see how they have used their culture and collective strength to survive the relentless demands for conformity and routinization imposed by the spread of industry, The goal is to write a new labor history, seen from "the bottom up."[5] Since the unorganized workers have been more numerous than the unionized, and since sources on them are often harder to locate, the task is challenging. There is the further difficulty of finding satisfactory analytical concepts for the "new" labor history.[6]

Should not this broader approach, which has opened new vistas for U.S. and European labor history, be equally relevant for Latin America?[7] Yes, but with an important qualification. It is true that historians of Latin American labor have also concentrated on unions, organizational leaders, and formal labor relations structures; but their research has been so scant that they have yet to produce an "orthodox" literature large enough to justify a full-scale revisionist reaction. For Latin America we need work on both fronts: increased research on unions and legal structures, as well as social history research and history written from the perspective of the workers, especially the unorganized. But it is essential to retain a critical attitude toward the revisionist scholarship on U.S. and European labor. Only in this way can Latin Americanists avoid the temptation to apply mechanically the revisionist gospel to the complex reality of Latin American working-class history.

The second revisionist trend in U.S., and especially European, labor historiography is the reexamination of national and international labor movements whose history has been neglected or distorted by previous interpretations. The most obvious cases are Anarchism, Anarcho-Syndicalism, and Syndicalism, as well as the international movements and organizations outside of the Comintern.[8] Past distortions have resulted from the historiographical (and political) dominance of the left exercised by Communist, especially Stalinist, historians and activists. As in the case of the revisionist turn to labor history from the "bottom up," this attempt to repair historiographical omissions and distortions came to the fore only in the 1960s.[9] Here, too, Latin Americanists have much to learn.

The second broad area of study offering potential help to historians of Latin American labor is labor economics. It is striking how seldom students of labor history, even that of the U.S. and Europe, pose the questions that labor economists routinely ask about contemporary labor systems. It is true that the theoretical orientation of labor economics has recently been in flux. The long-dominant (in the U.S. and Europe) neo-classical assumptions are under attack—leading to debates over the character and prevalence of "segmented" or "dual" labor markets[10]—yet labor historians have seldom turned to the concepts of any of these contending analytical approaches. Here again, students of Latin American labor history can benefit by looking closely at the rapidly growing body of research on the nature of labor markets in the developing world, including Latin America.[11] From that work historians can find ideas and questions of immediate value in their research and writing.

## The Neglect of Latin American Labor History: Causes and Cures

Until the mid-1960s Latin American labor history remained a curiously neglected field, with the exception of a few, relatively isolated, figures, such as Robert Alexander.[12] Most writing about Latin American history assigned a minor role to urban labor. Even where labor's role could not be ignored, as in the early Mexican Revolution or Perón's rise to power, the explanations have been markedly unsatisfactory. By contrast, rural workers seem to have fared better, perhaps in part because historians have correctly sought to acknowledge the overwhelmingly rural nature of Latin American societies. Yet how can we be sure of urban labor's relative unimportance until we have studied it carefully?

This relative neglect has begun to be corrected in recent years. A rising tide of books, articles, and anthologies indicates a broad-based interest.[13] The Fifth Meeting of Mexican and North American Historians (held in Pátzcuaro in October 1977), for example, was devoted entirely to labor history.[14] The Consejo Latinoamericano de Ciencias Sociales (CLACSO) has a commission of Latin American scholars specializing in labor movements, which has published conference papers.[15] The list of topics proposed by recently successful research grant applicants confirms the growing interest in labor history.[16] A new journal, *Latin American Perspectives,* of radical orientation, has published numerous articles on labor and labor movements.[17] The Latin American Program of the Woodrow Wilson International Center for Scholars (Smithsonian Institution, Washington, D.C.) held a workshop in late 1978 devoted to "Urban Working Class Culture and Social Protest in Latin America." The signs are unmistakable: a much-neglected topic has moved center stage.[18]

Why should Latin American labor history have been neglected? First, it should be noted that U.S. historians of Latin America have shared the elite-oriented approach generally dominant in North American historiography. The non-elites are much more difficult to study. Basic documentation is often lacking and the individuals remain faceless. Furthermore, the style and behavior of Latin American elites have proved more appealing to historians from abroad. Few foreign researchers have found themselves drawn to the grim world of the working class.[19] Among Latin Americans there has been more interest, but usually from militant intellectuals who were veterans of leftist organizational struggles. Although often informative, their accounts are usually apologies for their past positions, betraying the bitter struggles within the labor movement. Only since about the mid-1960s have Latin American scholars, and then primarily of the younger generation, published much on labor history.

This neglect has been especially noticeable until recently

for the years between 1914 and 1927, the great era of labor mobilization before 1945. It was the high point of the Anarchist, Anarcho-Syndicalist, and Syndicalist influence, when the capital cities of all the major Latin American nations were rocked by general strikes. Latin America suddenly seemed to be joining the class confrontations shaking Germany and Russia, as well as the U.S. and much of the rest of Europe.[20] It is at these critical moments—mass protests, general strikes, intensified ties between the unionized and the nonunionized—that we can learn much about the nature of the working class, its organizations, the manner in which the dominant elites chose to respond. Yet this high tide of Anarchist and Syndicalist mobilization has remained a misunderstood chapter of Latin American history. The problem stems in part from a heavy dependence on monographs or memoirs by participants. In Argentina, for example, accounts by former Anarchists and Anarcho-Syndicalists are numerous, but for obvious reasons must be used with caution. In Brazil the Anarchists produced fewer works, and in Chile practically none. In all three countries, however, Communist authors have published extensively, often furnishing the most widely read accounts. As a result, the role of Communist activists is especially well known. Yet these authors have often rewritten history in order to identify, according to prevailing dogmas at the time of writing, the rising proletariat, for whom the Communist parties would furnish the leaders. Given the fact that Anarchist, Anarcho-Syndicalist, and Syndicalist-led movements faded rapidly in the 1920s, Communists could more easily argue that such a fate was the inevitable result of an inappropriately conceived ("petit bourgeois") and incompetently applied (suicidal general strikes) labor ideology.[21] In view of the bitter struggles of the 1920s between Anarchists and Communists in all three countries, accounts by the latter obviously must be handled carefully.

There is another possible explanation for the neglect of Latin American labor history. Perhaps labor, especially organized labor, deserves its neglect. Advocates of this view, probably still a majority among scholars, argue that these movements have been too weak and divided to be important. Where appearing to play a significant role, they have been mere instruments for a caudillo, often in the guise of a populist, such as Juan Perón, Getúlio Vargas, or Victor Haya de la Torre. By this logic, labor was never to play in Latin America a role analogous to the one it played at crucial moments in the history of the North Atlantic industrial economies. Any initiatives that benefited labor (welfare systems) or helped to organize it (labor codes) are seen as unilateral moves by shrewd politicians who stayed ahead of labor organizers and thereby proved able, especially in Brazil, to co-opt the fledgling movements. In short, labor never attained the strength to bring its collective weight to bear within a pluralistic social structure.[22]

There is a third possible explanation, which applies especially to North American historians and social scientists. Labor movements in Latin America generally have differed greatly from their U.S. counterparts. In the U.S., unions usually developed as "bread-and-butter" organizations—concentrating on immediate material gains for the members.[23] That meant focusing on the employer and the place of employment. Although political activism by U.S. labor unions has increased since 1945, it has seldom approached the degree of "politicization" common in Latin America. Latin American deviance from the North American model disturbed government and labor union circles in the U.S. Many genuinely believed (and still believe) that all groups in Latin America would benefit from union concentration on job-related issues. That emphasis would make possible, they thought, at least a partial repetition of the pattern of successful pluralistic bargaining typical of the developed economies.[24] Often these observers also worried that the politicized unions of Latin America would fall under the control of radically anti-U.S. leaders —Communists or militant nationalists. Given the Cold War climate in which U.S. elites have operated since 1946, that worry was a serious factor. A reorientation of Latin American labor movements away from political adventuring would therefore serve the dual purpose of promoting healthier economic development and helping strengthen the Western Hemisphere against inroads by the ideological and strategic enemy, the U.S.S.R. The net effect of this worry was to distort analysis of Latin American labor history by concentrating on how unions could be changed, rather than understanding how the workers had come to act as they did, and how the elite reaction had established the subsequent framework of labor relations.[25]

Given the reasons for past neglect, why should there be an upsurge of interest now? One reason is the recent course of events in Latin America. The last fifteen years have brought a wave of military coups, frequently inflicting brutal repression of a kind few observers in the early 1960s would have thought possible. A key target for this repression has been organized labor. The Chilean military, since seizing power in September 1973, has regarded unions and union leaders as among the most dangerous enemies of the state. The junta's repressive assault on organized labor, killing thousands in the weeks following the coup, has no parallel in the modern history of major Latin American nations. The Chilean junta clearly fears labor as a powerful actor, and apparently will take any steps considered necessary to keep it under control.[26]

Argentina offers another interesting case. Despite the strenuous efforts of every government between Perón's overthrow in 1955 and his re-election in 1973, the Peronist movement, largely based on urban labor, survived as one of the most powerful participants in Argentine politics. One factor which helped maintain Peronist solidarity was the recurring cycle of economic stabilization attempts, which invariably resulted in falling real wage rates and attempts to reduce the work force on the deficit-ridden government railway system. The stabilization programs of Arturo Frondizi (1958–1962) and Juan Carlos Ongania (1966–1970), for example, both met stiff worker resistance.[27]

The other major nation of South America, Brazil, might at first seem an exception to this pattern. Had not Getúlio Vargas, during his authoritarian Estado Nôvo (1937–1945), created one of the most easily controllable labor movements? It is certainly true that Brazilian labor never attained the level of institutional autonomy, political consciousness, and success in influencing political events that was achieved by Argentine and Chilean labor. Yet it is worth remembering that it was President João Goulart's unwillingness to renounce his ties with militant labor leaders that helped convince important "legalist" Army commanders to join the coup to oust him in 1964. Not coincidentally, it was a challenge from industrial workers in 1968, led by wildcat leaders in Minas Gerais and São Paulo, that helped greatly to precipitate the "coup within a coup," institutionalizing a more authoritarian regime.[28] Government surveillance of Brazilian unions has remained extremely rigorous since then,[29] although with a relative easing in 1978. The pattern of conflict is unambiguous. Organized labor in all three countries is seen by those in power—military officers and their technocratic civilian collaborators—as a dangerous source of opposition.

How could this have come about? How have Latin American workers, once considered eminently manipulable, been able to frighten the guardians of national security? This historical puzzle, arising out of the current political facts of life, has helped to stir interest in the history of Latin American labor.

The upsurge of U.S. academic interest in this area also owes much to the changing assumptions of U.S. academics themselves. The trend has been steadily away from the once-dominant liberal developmentalist assumptions.[30] In part, reality has forced scholars to rethink their politico-ideological positions. The liberal developmentalist logic of the Alliance for Progress, for example, has been rendered irrelevant by the tide of authoritarian takeovers since the early 1960s. Contributing to that tide was one element of U.S. Latin American policy—the active support and encouragement of the "counter-insurgency" security forces, police, and military. Most U.S. liberals had accepted the argument that reformist governments needed to be able to defend themselves against armed insurrectionaries. As it turned out, however, the security forces became the government (or the dominant force within the government), with reformist regimes little more than a dim memory. In some cases the U.S. government tried to induce Latin American labor leaders to "destabilize" regimes disliked by the U.S. government. Seeing this documented in practice, as in the financing of some of former Chilean Presi-

dent Salvador Allende's most effective opponents (truckers), ←
has sobered academics who earlier regarded the charges of
U.S. complicity in coups to have been insufficiently proven.[31]
In short, many liberal academics, like many other liberal
Americans, have finally had to come to terms with the darker
side of the interventionism inherent in John F. Kennedy's am- ←
bitious offensive in Latin America.

This shift in ideological orientation of U.S. Latin Americanists has been reinforced by wider trends in North American academic circles. The younger generation of social science
area specialists has proved more ideologically heterogeneous
than its elders. The influence of Marxist, or, more accurately,
Marxian, ideas has grown.[32] The wide acceptance of differing
versions of "dependency" as an explanatory model is a further
indicator. The increased influence of Marxian analysis has
brought a much stronger interest in the working class, which
is assigned a central role in the classic Marxist prognosis.[33]
Taken together, these ideological trends among U.S. Latin
Americanists help further explain the boomlet in Latin American labor history. That trend is perhaps even more evident in
Western Europe, where British, West German, and French
social scientists specializing in Latin America have emphasized class analysis as the key to understanding modern Latin
America.[34] Finally, this historiographical trend has captured
the majority of social scientists trained *within* Latin America
in the last several decades. Thus the shift in ideological climate among Latin Americanists has been worldwide; one
spin-off has been greater attention to the historical role of
labor and labor movements in modern Latin America.

How far has this increased research and publication
brought us? Is the existing information—including quantitative data and documented monographs—sufficient to serve
as the base for comparative study? Only a few years ago, the
answer would have been no. The book-length syntheses available until recently are all seriously deficient, largely because
their authors attempt to generalize too much on the basis of
inadequate research literature. The result has been superficial,
and therefore seriously misleading, analysis. That situation
has changed. The recent spurt in research has created a more

secure base for carefully formulated, if necessarily tentative, comparative analysis. Done with care, such analysis can prove useful in the continuing research effort, which is unlikely to diminish. Because of this upsurge of interest, it is especially important to raise basic questions about assumptions and methodology.

Fortunately there are now available some excellent explorations in establishing typologies and comparative categories for the analysis of labor and labor's role in Latin America. All deserve careful study and discussion. I shall mention three, although they by no means exhaust the field. The most ambitious is J. Samuel Valenzuela's proposed conceptual framework for analyzing labor movements, elaborated as an introductory chapter to his comparative study, now in progress, of the evolution of the Chilean and French labor movements. A second overview, by Ruth and David Collier, is restricted to Latin America and focuses on the varying degree to which governments have mixed "inducements" and "constraints" in attempting to control the relationship between labor and the state by means of corporatist structures. A third survey, by Elizabeth Jelin, analyzes recent scholarship on the complex web of factors such as social background of workers, aspirations and class consciousness, economic structures and ideologies.[35]

This essay is an examination of one aspect of one chapter in Latin American labor history: how the reaction of ruling elites to the challenge of the largely Anarchist-led urban labor mobilization in Argentina, Brazil, and Chile in the early 1920s has influenced the shape of labor relations in our own day. Such an essay runs obvious risks. Concentrating on a single theme makes it difficult to maintain perspective on the total context in which elite-worker interaction occurred. How can that relationship be understood apart from an examination of the general lines of class conflict? How can we assess the role of organized labor without knowing the level of economic development and the principal characteristics of the labor market? How can we analyze elite reactions without an intimate knowledge of the socioeconomic and political relationships within the ruling elites? In short, any attempt at comparative historical analysis of the labor relations systems at this stage of historical knowledge must be tentative.

Comparative history is always risky. The drawing of comparisons invariably brings oversimplifications and therefore distortions. Yet comparative analysis can also raise questions that a single-country focus might miss. Within the Third World, Latin America has the advantage of presenting an array of independent countries that share basic characteristics— language, culture, colonial past, economic development— while at the same time exhibiting significant differences. With due attention to both similarities and differences, we should be able to suggest lines of analysis that will enable us to understand the particular cases better. This is especially true in the area of labor history, where the parallels in Latin America are often so striking.[36]

## The 1920s—Fateful Precedents

It is necessary to begin by examining briefly the present-day (late 1978) conditions for urban organized labor in Latin America, since so many of the current questions about labor history have been prompted by the recent fate of unions. All three countries in question—Argentina, Brazil, and Chile—are currently ruled by the military, with the degree of civilian collaboration varying from Brazil, where it is greatest, to Chile, where it is least. In all cases the most important decisions are made by the top ranks of military officers. One of the military's greatest concerns has been organized labor. Each military-dominated government has assumed the power to control decisions concerning labor's most vital interests— wages, working conditions, fringe benefits, and rights to organize. Labor has had to reconcile itself to the measures approved by the military-dominated government bureaucracies that set labor policies. Outright strikes have been virtually nonexistent in Chile since 1973 and in Brazil between 1968 and 1978. Moves to organize them in those countries have invited merciless repression, although some relaxation occurred in Brazil beginning in early 1978. Argentina's stronger tradition of union initiative has been harder to suppress, but labor leaders there have been forced to show great prudence also. In the area of labor relations, the three military regimes have approximated what, in a very different context, might be called a "command economy."

Why this heavy hand toward labor? Viewed from the short term, all three cases could be explained by the need to undertake unpopular anti-inflation policies. These regimes came to power when inflation and balance-of-payments deficits had made their economies dangerously vulnerable. In all three cases international credit, both public and private from the capitalist world, had been virtually closed off. All three regimes were required to launch stabilization programs. Since no capitalist country in recent years has succeeded in carrying out economic stabilization without producing a drop in real wages (usually very large), and since Argentina, Brazil, and Chile have all had extensive experience with organized labor's resistance to stabilization programs, these military governments might have been expected to seek strong control over labor.[37]

All three cases of antilabor policies, however, have more profound causes. These governments have proclaimed themselves "antipolitical"; all blame their countries' distress on the alleged incompetence, dishonesty, or treachery of politicians. They have been most aggressive against the radically leftist politicians and labor leaders. Few channels of political opposition are left open. Just as Chile was once the most democratic system, its military regime has been the most draconian, abolishing all political parties and burning the electoral rolls. The open pluralistic political competition for which that country was famous has been repudiated. Chile has entered an era "free" of politics.

In 1976, Argentina's military government took stern measures, although less sweeping than those in Chile. It suspended Congress and all political parties, thereby signifying a hiatus in competitive politics; but there was no wholesale repudiation. Brazil's military guardians, having come to power in a less radicalized political atmosphere than their counterparts in Argentina or Chile, also found themselves in their second year (1965) pushed to abolish the old political parties (replaced by two government-sanctioned new ones); they have allowed a limited range of continuing civilian participation, subject to intermittent intervention.

This South American scene contrasts sharply with the situation that prevailed in the early 1960s. At the onset of that decade the U.S. was promoting its Alliance for Progress, based on the assumption that economic development, social reform, and political democracy not only could but would blend harmoniously in Latin America. Meanwhile, the U.S. was to send capital and technology at increased levels. Everyone knew that much would depend on Latin American leadership. And in several countries skillful reformists were at the helm. Jânio Quadros in Brazil and Arturo Frondizi in Argentina seemed to promise the dynamic leadership that the Alliance demanded. Both were committed to open politics; unfortunately, both soon learned its perils. Quadros lasted only a few months, victimized by his own bad judgment. He dramatically announced his resignation, apparently to await a clamorous call back to power. Instead, his resignation was accepted. Frondizi lasted longer. But he, too, fell—the victim of a military coup in 1962 after an open election produced Peronist victories that the anti-Perón officers could not stomach.

It took longer for Chile to join the ranks of the authoritarians. Eduardo Frei's presidency (1964–1970) was a kind of coda for the Alliance for Progress. Chile was touted as a showcase for U.S. aid, which flowed at a per capita rate far higher than for any other Latin American nation. But Frei's reformism did not succeed in heading off the left. Allende's election and succession to the presidency in 1970 presented the greatest challenge ever to his country's much respected political sophistication. Chilean democracy could not withstand the heat of ideological polarization. Conspirators on the right liquidated the Unidad Popular government in a brutal coup (1973) that dramatized the military-labor confrontation far more painfully than had been the case in Argentina and Brazil.

Why did these three countries converge in the pattern of their politics? Why does the confrontation of soldier versus worker seem to symbolize such a large part of their current political dilemma? What clues can be found in the history of elite responses to the mobilization of urban labor?[38]

We need to examine the years of the Anarchist- and Anarcho-Syndicalist-led labor protest to understand the legal and political context of contemporary labor relations in Argentina, Brazil, and Chile. These years are important because all three countries saw the rise of militant urban working-class movements which seriously challenged both employers and the state by job actions, boycotts, and general strikes. Employers, as well as the ruling elites and governments in all three countries, had to respond. What we need to compare here are the similarities and differences in the patterns of interaction among employers, workers, and politicians, along with landowners, professionals, and the military. If there are similarities in urban labor's mobilization during the decade after the great protests began at the end of World War I, there were striking differences in the elite's response. In particular, we shall find that the legal framework of labor relations received much more attention in Chile than in Argentina and Brazil.

Our story starts at the beginning of this century. During the decade and a half between 1900 and World War I, Latin America benefited from the export-oriented economic growth made possible by the booming markets of the North Atlantic industrial economies. Brazil lived off coffee and natural rubber exports, Argentina off beef and grain, and Chile off nitrates. In all three countries, therefore, the money economy was sensitive to trends in the international economy, where exports earned the foreign exchange to buy badly needed imports. Any major shocks to the world economy would be bound to produce rapid and dramatic effects in the commercialized sectors. Although import-substituting industrialization had not gone far yet, factories existed in such sectors as textiles, leather goods, beverages, food processing, and construction materials. The most dynamic service sectors were transportation, government bureaucracy, commerce, and finance.[39]

The consequences of this economic structure for labor were several. First, because exports were crucial to all three economies, workers in the infrastructure supporting exports —especially railways and docks—stood at a vital point. Any work stoppage posed an immediate threat to the country's trade viability and therefore its capacity to import. Second, the relatively primitive state of industrialization meant that most workers were employed in very small firms, the overwhelming majority with less than twenty-five employees. Only a few industries, such as textiles, fit the modern image of huge factories with mass-production techniques. The unions in question were usually craft unions, or a recent outgrowth thereof. The exceptions were the rail workers, miners, and dockers, who, not coincidentally, were among the more militant workers.

For a thorough study of the cases of Argentina, Brazil, and Chile we need to start with an analysis of the state of labor relations systems in each country at the outset of our period— approximately 1900.[40] Were there formal contracts between employers and workers? If so, what kind of negotiating—if any—went into their creation? Did worker organizations exist? Were they legally recognized as representing workers? If not, was there de facto recognition and de facto negotiating? If negotiating occurred, even sporadically and outside a formal legal structure, what issues did it cover—wages? working conditions? fringe benefits?

A second important area is access to employment. How were workers recruited? Did employers have complete control over hiring? Or did workers—through collective action— share that control? Could they, for example, exercise any monopsonistic control?

If there were ongoing worker organizations, how were they structured and financed? What resources did they have to protect their members against reprisals from employer or government? At first glance it would seem that the market conditions were unfavorable for effective unionization, especially in Brazil and Chile. Were these not labor surplus economies, where labor resistance could presumably be bypassed by simply hiring new workers from the large pool available? If so, then as long as surplus labor was readily available, no worker action could be expected to succeed, unless the employer was, for some other reason, especially vulnerable to short-term disruption, or unless the government intervened and put pressure on the employers in a manner that the unfavorable market conditions prevented the workers from doing.[41]

We are therefore faced with a startling question at the outset of our inquiry: how was unionization possible at all in Latin America before 1945—or even *today*, in those economies where a labor surplus continues to exist? To ask that question is to suggest an obvious answer: perhaps there was *no* effective unionization before 1945—or perhaps even today in some of these countries. Perhaps we are merely asking about changing patterns of urban worker protest—through unions or other channels—but not union behavior in the sense in which that term is used in contemporary North America and Western Europe. That would appear to be the interpretation of scholars such as Adolf Sturmthal, who is frank in dismissing the possibility of genuine bargaining by labor when a huge unemployed and underemployed labor pool hangs over the market.[42]

If, on the other hand, we encounter cases where worker organization seems to have produced significant material concessions, we would expect to find three possible explanations: (1) the labor surplus did not exist; (2) a labor surplus existed, but was neutralized by the creation of a segmented labor market due to barriers to entry resulting from employer manipulation, monopsonistic employee behavior, or some societally imposed structure; or (3) there was government intervention—of one kind or another. Possibility (3) is considerably easier to research than (1) or (2). We shall need to keep all three possibilities in mind.

The questions posed above are second nature to specialists in industrial relations and labor economics. Yet they are not easy to answer for the history of the U.S. or Europe, let alone the Argentina, Brazil, and Chile of 1900. Obviously the answers will vary greatly by industry and locale. To paint a complete picture requires detailed, documented monographs on urban labor, industry by industry. For the most part, we lack industry studies, although we are now beginning to get well-researched studies of worker movements. As a result, for the essential background on the structure of labor relations in 1900 we must rely on a frequently inadequate secondary literature. Readers should remember that this will limit our ability to examine in depth the interaction of worker protest and elite response, especially as it concerns changes in the operational structure of labor relations. Readers should also remember that what follows is an exercise in traditional labor history—concentrating on unions and employer and government response to union mobilization. Largely neglected will be the nonunion efforts, especially those organized outside the workplace, such as the massive rent strike in Buenos Aires in 1907.[43] Neglected also are those many occasions of working-class action which were largely symbolic or fraternal, rather than politically or bargaining oriented.[44]

## Urban Labor Movements in Argentina, 1900–1930

Argentina is an interesting case because of the vigor of its early labor mobilization and the degree to which labor remained free of a state-imposed framework.[45] Although there were some impressive strike efforts in late-nineteenth-century Argentina, the significant organizational upsurge came after 1900. Between 1901 and 1910 the organized urban labor movement was dominated by leaders varyingly committed to the philosophical doctrines which bore the label of Anarchism. The government was worried enough by their strikes to push through passage of a Ley de Residencia in 1902, facilitating the deportation of foreign-born organizers. The reactionary, xenophobic lawmakers, who thought labor protest could be little more than the work of subversive foreigners, had a point, since so many of the Anarchists were aliens.[46]

Notwithstanding this reaction from most government politicians, one legislator, Joaquín V. González, sought in 1904 to contain and channel the labor protest through a general code for labor relations which he proposed to the Congress. González's initiative was met with rude opposition from both Conservatives and labor leaders. The former opposed in principle any recognition of labor's rights to organize, while the latter, led by the Anarchists, rejected it because they suspected that any government system would be manipulated against them. The combination was fortunate from the long-term standpoint of labor, because it prevented the early creation of a legal framework which might well have become a straitjacket on labor.

The accommodationists within the political elite were not discouraged, however, by the fate of the González bill. In 1907 the Congress created a Department of Labor, and invited the FORA (Federación Obrera Regional Argentina) and the UGT (Unión General de Trabajo), leading labor union confederations, to participate in the Tribunal designated to resolve labor conflicts. Both organizations "refused to support the 'corrupt bourgeois government' in this effort."[47] Once again, Argentine labor escaped incorporation into a government-controlled structure of labor relations.

Meanwhile, the Anarchists continued their effective organizing, especially among immigrant workers in Buenos Aires. A climax to their effort came in 1910. The government had mounted a great public celebration of the centennial of the declaration of Argentine independence. The Anarchist leaders saw their opportunity as well; they were determined to raise labor's voice in a mighty protest against what they saw as the farce of Argentine progress. It was not, however, a work-related action; it was a symbolic challenge. They could not have chosen a better issue on which to rouse the ire of both the oligarchy and the middle-class *porteños* (residents of Buenos Aires). Anarchist-led attempts at public manifestations were met with police charges. It was class warfare in a startling guise. The result was a total victory for the repressive forces. In the aftermath a new law was passed—the Ley de Defensa Social—giving the government virtual carte blanche to arrest and try labor organizers. The hunt was on for any and all leaders of the urban protest movement. The Anarchists, who still held the initiative among the leadership of the urban unions, became the prime targets. The following years were dark for the labor movement. Anarchist leaders were persecuted, harassed, imprisoned, and deported. It was the death knell of the Anarchist movement, although not all contemporaries could yet perceive it.

Amid this repression, 1912 brought a harbinger of political change. That year the Congress enacted the Sáenz Peña Law, which significantly broadened the franchise. For the first time the vote was opened to the articulate and frustrated middle-sector citizens whose supreme political expression was the Radical Party.[48] This reform enabled the well-organized Radical Party to win the presidential election of 1916 and triumphantly install its leader, Hipólito Yrigoyen, in office. In contrast with preceding governments, the Radical regime did not routinely resort to the use of police to break up strikes. Their attitude was a mixture of genuine concern for the material fate of the working classes and an interest in finding votes in their quest to displace the Conservatives as Argentina's governing party. In some negotiating conflicts, the Yrigoyen government proved sympathetic to labor. From the labor standpoint it was an incremental improvement, dependent on continued government sympathy case by case. Significantly, the Radicals made no attempt to create a new legal framework for labor relations.

Radical forbearance toward labor was stretched to the breaking point, however, during the monumental labor protest of 1918–1919. It was a moment when workers throughout the Western world—from Berlin to Turin, from Chicago to Lima, from São Paulo to Buenos Aires, rose in general strikes against their employers *and* the state. It was a confluence of specific grievances and generalized hostility. It was also one of those moments when spontaneous protest caught even the militant organizers by surprise. Most of the strikers and demonstrators belonged to no union, suggesting a growing class consciousness. In Argentina, as elsewhere in Latin America, worker discontent was fueled by the sharp drop in real wage rates resulting from the inflation of World War I. Prices, especially of food, had risen quickly (because of European demand), while wages had lagged. The resulting squeeze was deeply felt by the urban workers in Buenos Aires, as elsewhere in the major cities of Latin America. A series of individual union strikes in Buenos Aires in late 1918 and early 1919 stimulated other union leaders—mostly Syndicalist—to opt for a general strike—the long-cherished Syndicalist instrument for bringing down the bourgeois state. The result was the Semana Trágica, in which several hundred strikers were cut down in the streets by police. The Radical government was forced into the role of a bourgeois repressive regime. Part of the pressure in that direction came from a newly formed ultra-rightist civilian paramilitary movement, the Liga Patriótica Argentina, fed by middle- and upper-class fear and fury toward the popular challenge.[49] The Liga took to the streets to attack the workers, thereby promoting naked class warfare. The contradiction in the middle-class "opening" to the working class became evident. Once again the labor leadership was sharply repressed. The Syndicalists suffered heavily, as did the last remnants of the Anarchist leadership.

After 1919 the Argentine labor movement was to come under new leadership. The Anarchists, gravely weakened before 1919, faded definitively. The Syndicalists, with a better chance for survival, now faced competition from those who were to promote the cause of the Second International. Competition came also from the Socialists, a political current virtually absent elsewhere in Latin America.[50] Their appearance in Argentina at this point was proof that Argentina was the most advanced nation in Latin America, at least if one judged by the timing of the appearance of Socialist parties in the chronology of European political development. The Socialists claimed to offer a means for workers to improve their material conditions by direct leverage on the established political system. By their vote, argued the Socialists, urban workers (little attention was paid to rural workers) could force the ruling elites to make concessions to them. But the Socialists had made only sporadic and ineffective efforts to gain influence in the unions, where the Syndicalists and Communists shared control.

Labor organization in the early 1920s was influenced by a further factor: the material conditions for urban workers improved dramatically after the Semana Trágica. Real wage rates, as best we can determine, increased steadily during the decade—not, however, because of union pressure. On the contrary, rising wages may have undermined unionization. The remainder of the 1920s saw Argentine labor continue in a pluralistic world of competition among labor organizers, with no definitive legal framework governing labor relations. In short, Argentine labor arrived at 1930 free from a government-imposed labor code which might have imprisoned it within a web of legal and political restrictions.

## Urban Labor Movements in Brazil, 1900–1930

Brazil, although less advanced economically before 1930 than Argentina, also produced an urban labor movement that alarmed the elite, so fond of describing Brazilian society as immune to the class conflict that plagued other countries.[51] As in Argentina, there was organized activity before 1900 but the workers' associations that had appeared were vulnerable and impermanent. After 1902, organization increased, centering in the skilled trades, construction, and transport sectors. This phase climaxed in the "First Labor Conference" of 1906, where the Anarcho-Syndicalists established a dominance they were to retain until 1920. Union growth continued steadily until 1908, although the scale of labor organization was modest. There had been little success, for example, in textiles, by far the largest industry. In 1908 a four-year decline set in, apparently due in part to the economic downturn occasioned by a slump in the world economy.

As in Argentina, the Anarchist leadership included many aliens.[52] The Brazilian political elite seized on this fact, resorting to deportation as a major weapon. In 1907 a new deportation law was passed, facilitating repression. Although there had been a brief resurgence of labor organization in 1912–1913, with the Second Labor Congress held in 1913, a severe recession took hold of the Brazilian economy in the latter year, and 1913 also saw a tightening of the deportation regulations. Up to 1917, the year the Bolshevik revolution cast its shadow over Europe, the Brazilian urban labor movement had offered little threat to the established order.

The war years presented urban workers with a grave problem: rapidly rising prices, especially of food, which severely reduced their real wages. It gave them a material incentive for listening to the Anarcho-Syndicalist leaders, who called for strikes in Rio and São Paulo. The years 1917–1920 brought a surge of strikes such as Brazil had never known. They began in São Paulo in mid-1917. Worker dissatisfaction spread through the textile industry and burst out in July, when textile workers demanded wage increases. The strike wave then spread to the breweries. Much of the protest was spontaneous. The leadership sought to expand the protest into a more general "political" strike, perhaps because the degree of worker militancy had caught them partly by surprise and they were scrambling to catch up. The strike spread to Rio, where the employers proved less conciliatory. In São Paulo, however, the workers won significant concessions from the employers, who negotiated via a commission of journalists. (Unfortunately, the labor leadership had no way of insuring compliance with the agreements, which many employers later chose to ignore.)

By the end of 1918 the Anarchist leadership in Rio had become emboldened by the prospect of worker militancy. They secretly planned a huge protest, which they hoped would lead to an insurrection that would topple the established political order. It was a moment in which the utopian political vision of the Anarchists overcame their experience with workplace-centered strike tactics. The plot was discovered, the leaders arrested, and the protest aborted.

The following year, 1919, brought a new wave of strike activity. In May, workers at the São Paulo factory of Francisco Matarazzo launched a strike, touching off a chain reaction of strikes across the city. What began as an "economic" strike movement was again transformed, by October, into an attempt at a general strike. Once more the Anarcho-Syndicalist leadership opted for what they planned to be a serious blow to the state. They sought to mobilize worker discontent over specific grievances—low wages, their late payment, poor working conditions, child labor, inadequate weekend and holiday provisions—into a challenge to the entire socioeconomic system. The results were disastrous. In the two years after the 1917 strike wave, both state and federal governments had prepared themselves for swifter and more effective repression. The workers were pathetically underprepared for direct confrontation. "Politicization" of the strike movement, given the relative power positions in 1919, was bound to preclude success on the "economic" issues over which the strikes had begun in May. In March 1920 the textile workers of both Rio and São Paulo attempted to mount general strikes. They received the full measure of repression the government had been readying. The strikes were broken and the systematic persecution of labor leaders began. The last gasp came in early 1921, when the maritime workers and the Anarcho-Syndicalist leaders of Rio called for another general strike. It was a dismal failure. The same year the Congress tightened the deportation law again, easing the way for summary removal of foreign-born labor organizers. The Anarchist leadership never recovered. They had succeeded in channeling worker discontent into a dramatic confrontation with employers, then with the State, embodied by the police and the military. The response they elicited was first non-recognition, then conciliation, and then repression. Yet they had shown that urban workers could be organized into collective action far more threatening than most Brazilian employers or politicians would have dreamed possible before World War I.

The decade of the 1920s found organized labor in Brazil weak and on the defensive.[53] The Anarcho-Syndicalist leadership never recovered from the repression provoked by the 1917–1920 strike effort. Union membership plummeted. Strikes were infrequent and almost invariably costly failures. Unlike Argentina, which enjoyed steady economic prosperity, Brazil suffered a continuing industrial crisis during the 1920s. Data indicate that a large pool of labor, swollen by foreign immigrants and in-migrants from the rural sector, hung over the market, creating an unfavorable economic context.

The political climate could hardly have been worse. The repression unleashed in 1919–1920 continued through the decade. In part, labor organizers were caught in the cross fire of an intra-elite struggle. During its last decade the "Old Republic" (1889–1930) was wracked by political revolt. Prominent among the rebels were younger military officers (the Tenentes), who took up arms in 1922 (Rio), 1924 (São Paulo and Rio Grande do Sul), and 1924–1927 (the rebel Coluna

Prestes [Prestes Column]). The government countered the rebel challenge by continuous resort to the "state of siege" provision in the Constitution. Although aimed primarily at the opposition from within the elite, use of these arbitrary powers was readily extended to labor organizers as well. During these same years a series of ad hoc decrees and laws created a partial system of labor relations, restricted to a few sectors (such as railway workers and port workers), along with scattered social welfare laws (compensation for accidents, child labor regulations).[54]

Especially important to note is the fact that Brazil did not have a middle-sector political movement that found it necessary to seek worker support in a struggle for power with the incumbent political oligarchy. The Tenentes lacked any clearly articulated position on the role of the working class, as became evident with the advent of the Revolution of 1930.[55] The urban middle sectors, strongest in Rio and São Paulo, remained susceptible to the scare tactics of employers and reactionary politicians. There was no significant group within the elite seeking to incorporate labor into the established structure. Instead, the challenge mounted by the Anarcho-Syndicalist-led workers in 1917–1920 had been met in two ways: (1) repression, and (2) provision of minimal working conditions and social welfare laws (compensation for accidents, etc.) for a few critical economic sectors, such as railway and port workers. Like Argentina, Brazil reached 1930 without any systematic labor-relations system codified in law.

Meanwhile, during the 1920s the Communists had steadily replaced the Anarcho-Syndicalists in union leadership.[56] In fact, much of the slowly growing membership of the Brazilian Communist Party (founded in 1922) came from the waning ranks of the Anarchists. Whatever their virtues, the Communists lacked commitment to, and effectiveness at, grass-roots union organizing. Throughout the 1920s the Communists and Anarchists battled bitterly—in no other Latin American Communist Party was there such a strong influx of ex-Anarchists, and nowhere else were there such recriminations over alleged backsliding by these converts. As a result, too few energies were left for the hard work of worker recruitment and organization.

## Urban Labor Movements in Chile, 1900–1930

In Chile, as in Argentina and Brazil, viable labor unions did not appear on the scene before the turn of the century, although there had been some significant strikes in the 1890s.[57] The first phase of effective strike activity came in 1905–1908, although the "resistance societies" (mutual assistance groups) had launched some successful strike actions earlier in the decade. Such groups were strongest among skilled workers. In June 1907 they mounted a large-scale general strike in Santiago and won a number of concessions. December of that year, however, brought violence. In the northern port of Iquique, striking nitrate workers and their families confronted army troops and fell by the hundreds in what bore all the marks of a massacre. A wave of repression struck the urban working-class movement. Workers were also hit hard by an economic recession. Only in 1909 could labor organizers begin seriously rebuilding their movement. For the next five years there was steady progress, with the Anarcho-Syndicalists providing most of the leadership. A series of successful strikes followed, including a general strike in October 1913 in the port city of Valparaiso, where union structure was more centralized than in Santiago. But 1914 began another very difficult period for workers, who were hit by rising prices, which rapidly eroded the purchasing power of workers' take-home pay. Santiago's labor supply increased in 1914 (unemployed nitrate workers from the north resettled in Santiago), further weakening workers' bargaining power. The only significant strike action was by rail workers in 1916, but they were a case apart, since they enjoyed an especially favorable bargaining position.

Labor organization began to revive in 1917. The economy was in an upswing, strengthening labor's hand. Inflation was again cutting into real wages, making workers receptive to the organizers' appeals. For the next three years unionization grew steadily, despite the fact that Chilean law did not recognize labor unions, thus placing them in an extralegal limbo. It was an era of pragmatic leadership, with emphasis on the fundamentals of organization-building; ideological differences were downplayed. May Day rallies in 1917 and 1918, for example, were huge successes, symbolizing the ability of Anarcho-Syndicalists, Anarcho-Communists, Socialists, and reformists to work together effectively. This growth of labor strength did not sit well with the incumbent political oligarchy, nor with the middle sectors. As in Argentina and Brazil, the elite thought worker discontent must have been caused by foreign agitators. In 1918 the Congress passed a Ley de Residencia, much like the Argentine and Brazilian laws. It was designed to rid the country of aliens who were active labor organizers. But the politicians had not done their homework. Chile had virtually no such aliens. Much to the disappointment of the elite, the deportation strategy would not work in Chile.

This curious fact is worth further consideration. As in Argentina and Brazil during the years before 1920, the Anarchists and Anarcho-Syndicalists predominated, although the Socialists had surprising power. Unlike those cases, however, the Anarcho-Syndicalists in Chile were overwhelmingly home-grown. Whatever the situation in Argentina and Brazil, Anarcho-Syndicalism in Chile was not a movement aimed at immigrant workers and led by foreign-born organizers. European immigration had been insignificant in Chile, except for Germans in the south, who were hardly accessible to urban-based organizers. Anarchist and Syndicalist ideas reached Chile via occasional visitors from Europe or North America, but more frequently through publications and contacts in Argentina. As a result, the Chilean labor organizers were less vulnerable to the attacks of reactionary nationalists who attributed labor unrest to foreign "subversives." That did not, however, stop such attacks from being made; they were made, continuously. But it does warn us not to rely too heavily on the nationality of the workers as an explanation for the strength of Anarchist and Syndicalist doctrines and leadership in Latin America.

The year 1919 was the high point of this period of successful labor mobilization. In January and February the union leaders staged huge rallies in Santiago to protest the high prices brought by wartime inflation. In August there was another mammoth demonstration, with 100,000 participants marching past the presidential palace. Here was a case of more broadly based working-class protest, which included many demonstrators who were not union members. It seemed to indicate a significant state of class consciousness. The resulting confidence of labor leaders, both Anarcho-Syndicalist and IWW, led them to attempt a general strike in Santiago in aid of brewery workers, whose current strike was foundering. The general strike was called for September; it was unsuccessful in pressuring the brewery owners, whose workers returned in defeat. This attempt at class solidarity had failed in its immediate purpose, and the effect on worker morale was negative. By early 1920, strikes were becoming less frequent. Surprisingly enough, government reaction to strikers had been relatively moderate since the labor resurgence began in 1917. In December of that year an executive edict (the Yáñez Decree) set up a mediating role for government in stalemated labor conflicts. Although rejected in principle by Anarchist and Syndicalist leaders, it was heavily used, often to labor's benefit, in 1918 and 1919. That pattern continued for the first half of 1920, in part because the government did not wish to poison the atmosphere for an important upcoming presidential election, scheduled for June.

Chile, like Argentina, had liberalized the franchise enough to open the door to significant middle-sector political participation, a process far less advanced in Brazil. The number of enfranchised working-class citizens, although still small, had begun to attract the attention of Chilean bourgeois politicians soon after the turn of the century, especially in Santiago. Their votes could be significant, especially in cases where the voting was divided among many parties, as was the case in Chile. The political leader who saw this most clearly was Arturo Alessandri, running for President in 1920. He made a passionate appeal to urban voters, including workers, whom he promised to favor both by negotiating labor conflicts and by creating a modern system of social welfare. Alessandri represented an "enlightened" middle-sector view —accepting the inevitability of working-class participation in the society and the economy, while also hoping to channel it into controllable lines of action. The model he proposed was a modified corporatist structure, which would legitimize unions, while also locating them within an intricate legal framework that gave final control to the government.[58]

Alessandri narrowly won the election. With this democratic exercise now over, the incumbent government of President Juan Luis Sanfuentes felt free to respond to the labor challenge. In July, workers felt the onslaught of the Ligas Patrióticas, the paramilitary street activists recruited from right-wing middle- and upper-class families. Systematic government repression now began. Arrest and imprisonment faced virtually all Anarcho-Syndicalist and other leaders who did not flee into exile or find hiding inside the country. The leaderless workers were further demoralized by a wave of lockouts, in which employers took back many of the concessions made in the years from 1917 to 1920.

— Yet there was hope that the government attitude would change when Alessandri assumed office. So it did. For the first half of 1921 the Alessandri government intervened (under authority of the Yáñez Decree) in a number of strikes, favoring workers in their mediation. But labor conflict turned violent. Alessandri found himself attacked from all sides—from the right for having shown labor too much sympathy and from the left for not doing enough to restrain the aggressive employer tactics. In July 1921, Alessandri intervened in a bitter tram strike in Santiago, helping the company to strike-break. From August to October there was a wave of successful lockouts. By the end of 1921, the government had reverted to a policy of systematic repression.

A string of lockouts, accompanied by the creation of company unions, continued through 1922 and 1923. In early 1922 the coal miners struck. An attempted general strike failed to help them. The employers and the government, now very confident, had the upper hand. It was also the time of a great increase in the ideological orientation of the labor organizations.

Battles between Anarcho-Syndicalists and Communists became open and bitter. Although the best-organized single labor group, the FOCh (Federación Obrera de Chile) came under complete Communist leadership, the Anarcho-Syndicalists continued to control most of the unions in Santiago and Valparaiso.

While organized labor was struggling against adverse economic and political conditions, President Alessandri pressed for adoption of his proposed labor code and social welfare package, which had been introduced in Congress in 1921. The Conservatives had presented their own proposal in 1919. They were now determined to block the Liberal initiative, and they had the strength in Congress to do so. Many Conservatives undoubtedly preferred the status quo—in which unions had no legal status and were therefore exposed to continuous assaults from both employers and government. Furthermore, the Conservatives feared that the Liberals might generate a new voter following among urban workers. The stand-off between the Liberal President and the Conservative Congress continued until 1924. In that year the military broke the impasse, as a military junta took partial control of the government in early September, soon forcing Alessandri out of the presidency.[59] Only three days after the rebellious military had issued a manifesto listing legislative demands, the Congress dutifully approved every one. Included was a package of measures aimed at labor, the most important being an elaborate labor code.

The new code incorporated elements of competing proposals previously put forward by the Liberals and the Conservatives. On one point, however, they differed little: both subjected unions to very close supervision by the government. Neither was designed to encourage competitive unionization in a pluralistic framework. There was to be exclusive representation granted to the union recognized by the government. Labor disputes were to be resolved by government tribunal and commission. The package of measures also included additions to the very advanced (for the era) programs of medical care, vacations, and pensions. In short, Chile followed the Bismarckian model of the 1880s in establishing an elaborate system of social welfare benefits. As in the German Empire, this social advance was *not* the product of a political process in which the workers could play a direct role. It was a preemptive move by the government, under military pressure, to head off further independent mobilization by workers' organizations. This apparently progressive step resulted directly from the arbitrary action of a government cadre that had much to fear from worker mobilization—the military officer corps.

The imposition of the labor code coincided with a resurgence of labor conflict. An upturn in the economy had tightened the labor supply, and rising prices gave workers reason to demand wage raises. Leadership was active across the ideological spectrum: Anarcho-Syndicalist (still the strongest), Communist, and reformist (those ready to accommodate the labor movement to government-channeled concessions and controls). Meanwhile, conflict between the military and Alessandri had led the President to take a leave abroad, from which he was recalled after a second military coup in January 1925. At this point, ironically, the newly predominant military felt that they needed both Alessandri and urban labor support, as they saw the precariousness of their legitimacy. This new military government intervened frequently in strikes, usually to the benefit of the workers. It seemed that organized labor might be on the verge of gaining power; some even thought the revolution was at hand. Fear spread among the elite, who were acutely aware that they had lost control.

The revolution was not at hand. Alessandri returned from his leave in March 1925 and soon delivered another lesson on the vulnerability of organized labor. The government position turned more repressive in a clash with nitrate workers in June 1925. For the next two years labor found itself battling not only government hostility but also economic recession, with its inevitable labor surplus. In January 1927 labor leadership ill-advisedly attempted a general strike. Labor's divisions became all too obvious; the strike failed. In February, Colonel Carlos Ibáñez del Campo won de facto control of the government and was shortly thereafter confirmed in the presidency by a popular election; he then embarked on a virtual dictatorship. In the wake of his coup, labor leaders became a prime target. Massive arrests and imprisonments shattered the union movement. The government's dual response to the urban challenge was now complete. The all-encompassing labor code of 1924 was in place, and the long arm of military and police repression had silenced the independent voices among the workers.

## The Post-Anarchist Legacy

What happened in these three countries after the largely Anarchist-led challenge had been defeated? In Chile, Colonel Ibáñez presided over a dictatorial regime (1927–1931) that resorted to repression of independent labor leaders and attempted to create a cadre of new pro-government leaders. With the end of the Ibáñez regime in 1931, that effort failed, and Chile began its long (by Latin American standards) experiment in union democracy. Union elections were fiercely contested, but reasonably honest. Here the functioning of the corporatist-designed structure helped in the emergence of union leaders with genuine followings, as the government-appointed inspectors, empowered to certify election results, proved relatively neutral. The Communists, who had been led by the redoubtable figure of Luis Emilio Recabarren until his suicide in late 1924, found competition for worker leadership from a new revolutionary party which had appeared—the Socialist Party, whose founders included many former Anarchist leaders.[60] In 1938 a Popular Front government, including Communists, Socialists, and Radicals, was able to reach power. Thus the military (and cooperating elites) had succeeded in containing the potential for significant class confrontation within the labor relations system, but had failed to prevent militant left-wing parties from capturing the voting loyalty of a large segment of organized urban workers. Furthermore, the links between unions and left-wing political parties became very close.[61] As a result of this legitimation of democratic mobilization on the left, the "social question" was to become increasingly the heart of political conflict. In the 1960s, concern over it led to Frei's ambitious attempt at reformism, and then to Allende's attempt at social revolution within the pluralistic political system. The price paid for the ultimate failure of both attempts was heavy. It returned Chile to the confrontation of soldier and worker that the preemptive measures of 1924–1927 were to have headed off.

In Argentina, Radical rule ended in 1930, when a military coup deposed the aged Yrigoyen and brought first General José Felix Uriburu and then General Juan B. Justo to power. In fact, the Conservative Party ruled from behind the scenes, and a subsequent resurgence of Radical influence did not change the unsympathetic attitude toward labor which had typified all the governments since the early 1920s.[62]

Argentina thus reached the eve of World War II without a systematic labor code or comprehensive social welfare legislation. Labor unions continued to exist and had maintained organizational strength since the dark days of the mid-1920s. The workers had not, however, found a political voice comparable to that of labor in Chile. The Communist Party in Argentina had remained small, under steady government harassment. There was a Socialist Party, cast more on the lines of a European Social Democratic party than on the mold of the revolutionary Socialist Party in Chile. In Argentina it had succeeded in building a working-class following in Buenos Aires, although its success elsewhere in the country was extremely limited. In sum, organized urban workers in Argentina had neither a legitimized labor relations system nor a militant political champion. All that was to change in 1943.

In 1943 Colonel Juan Perón started his meteoric rise to power, beginning in the National Labor Department, of which he was named the Director.[63] Perón soon moved into the political vacuum surrounding labor. His governments after 1945 were to provide both a fully articulated labor system officially sanctioned by the government and a comprehensive program of social welfare benefits. Perón was not, however, acting alone. He represented a major current of opinion among Army officers, who were concerned over the growth of organized urban labor. They feared the political—and perhaps even military— potential of these masses. They scorned the civilian politicians for having merely postponed the inevitable acknowledgment of this rising social force. The specter of possible radicalization, even Bolshevism, seemed a real threat. Because Perón was a thoroughly unoriginal thinker, he could be a superbly effective public personality representing a South American adaptation of some elements of European, especially Italian, Fascism. Earlier, Perón had served as a military attaché in Rome; he was a known admirer of Mussolini. Although the regime which lasted from the coup of 1943 until the coup of 1955 went through several stages with an ever greater cult of personality, we should not lose sight of the fact that the motivation of a large part of the GOU (Grupo de Oficiales Unidos)—the group of officers which was the most important force behind the 1943 coup—closely resembled that of the Chilean junta of 1924–1927. Both wanted to pre-empt labor mobilization by creating a controllable labor relations system and to undercut independent working-class political organization by the imposition of social welfare benefits established by edict. In essence, the Argentine officers wanted to close off the avenues of independent professional and political action of the urban workers. The Argentine officers came to their reactionary task late, but with strong resolve.[64]

As history turned out, this military direction of worker organization resulted in a colossal cult of personality that was to overshadow Argentine politics for decades to follow. It is also important to acknowledge that Peronism brought enormous benefits—both material and psychological—to the urban working class. The true character of this extraordinary era was obscured by the stubborn unwillingness of many on the left to recognize that Perón was *not* simply a South American Fascist. Significantly, it was a military regime, led by General Alejandro Lanusse, that was finally driven, in 1973, to allow Perón back to govern Argentina. Yet the ghost failed to be exorcised.[65] Nor did Perón's death extinguish his charisma. Seen in historical perspective, however, what remains is a military initiative to save Argentina from the revolutionary left. Juan Perón is dead, Evita Perón is dead, and Isabelita Perón languishes under lengthening house arrest. All that remains is the familiar confrontation of soldier versus worker.

As in Chile, labor unions are intervened by military officers. For the moment, elections, as well as strikes, belong to the past.

In Brazil, as in Argentina, 1930 saw the military dislodge the incumbent civilian regime. One of the early acts of Getúlio Vargas, as Provisional President, was to create a separate Ministry of Labor, splitting it off from the Ministry of Commerce and Industry. Yet Brazilian labor, like Argentine labor, had reached the watershed of 1930 without any systematic labor relations system having been imposed. Equally important, the Vargas era began with the urban movement divided and weak.

The legally defined role of labor was to change greatly during the rule of Vargas. Further definition of labor's status was extensively discussed by the Provisional Government (1930–1934), and some measures were enacted in that period. At the time of the Constituent Assembly of 1933–1934, however, the present form of the labor relations framework still lay in the future. The leaders of the Assembly drew up a relatively flexible legal structure for unions, embodied in the Constitution of 1934, which facilitated an extraordinary upsurge in political activity in 1934–1935. Suddenly the left came to life, mobilized by the ANL (Aliança Nacional Libertadora), a popular front movement. Unfortunately for those labor leaders who favored the peaceful road, the Brazilian Communist Party was engaged in a two-pronged strategy: one was the legal effort of the ANL; the other was a conspiracy to carry out a coup within the Army. The latter was easily crushed in November 1935.[66] In the aftermath all leaders on the militant left were hunted to the ground. All leadership on the left had been discredited by a conspiracy that played into the hands of those planning their own coup: the authoritarian coup by Vargas with military sponsorship in November 1937. Here the Brazilian case converged with the Chilean and Argentine ones. It was during the Estado Nôvo (1937–1945) that the first systematic labor code was adopted. Once again, it was not the product of open political bargaining in which independent organized labor had an input; it was imposed by the executive.

The form of the Brazilian system (codified as the Consolidacão das Leis do Trabalho in 1943) was largely corporatist, similar in many details to the Chilean code. The principle of exclusive union representation was adopted, with total control over recognition of the legal union vested in the Ministry of Labor. The latter was also given power to supervise the finances and election of officers of the unions. An elaborate system of labor courts was created to handle grievances, and the right to strike was effectively denied.[67]

Although the Brazilian labor code may have resembled Chile's in some formal aspects—for example, only one union was permitted at plant level and government bureaucrats held the power to grant recognition—the application of the two codes was very different. In Chile, from the end of the Ibáñez dictatorship in 1931 until the beginning of the Augusto Pinochet dictatorship in 1973, genuine competition for union leadership prevailed, with members of revolutionary parties able to hold office and to promote close links with their parties. In Brazil, however, governments wielded a much heavier hand in the operation of the unions. In the years between the end of the Estado Nôvo in 1945 and the military coup of 1964, the Communist Party was legal for only two years (1945–1947). Its outlawing in 1947 coincided with a purge—via the corporatist controls provided by the labor code of 1943—of left-wing union leaders. The subsequent manipulation of union machinery by the Ministry of Labor guaranteed the continued absence of any leadership found objectionable by the government.

When Getúlio Vargas returned to the presidency in 1951, intervention by the Ministry of Labor eased, as the loyalty oath (atestado de ideología) for union officers was suspended. There followed an upsurge of spontaneous worker mobilization that contributed to a massive strike in São Paulo in 1953. The mobilization occurred in unofficial worker commissions, formed outside the government-controlled union structure. The workers won their immediate goal—a significant wage increase—but their newly formed commissions were soon absorbed into the official union machinery. The attempt to create a "parallel" union structure, with genuinely democratic choice of leadership, failed. Instead, the Ministry of Labor maintained its control until the early 1960s, when a new challenge was mounted, but it had not gone far when the coup of 1964 brought a massive crackdown on the left. Thus the corporatist machinery set up during the Estado Nôvo continued to serve its creators' purposes.[68]

It is important to understand that those architects of the corporatist system got their opportunity in 1943 only because the military had intervened in Brazilian politics. Although the Estado Nôvo was not a straightforward military junta, such as the Chilean regime of 1924–1927 or the Argentine government of 1943–1946, Vargas and his civilian advisors could never have held power without strong support—including recourse to arbitrary police and military action—from the Army. Officer support had been made all the more certain by the Communist uprising of November 1935. That would-be *putsch* gave ample ammunition to the antidemocratic leaders among the officers. Some, such as Generals Pedro Góes Monteiro and Eurico Dutra, were already known as sympathizers of the Axis regimes in Germany and Italy. Fascist ideas about controlling labor were therefore widespread in officer circles in Brazil, as they were among the GOU officers in Argentina.

Brazil differed from Argentina and Chile in an important way, however. In Chile, revolutionary political parties on the left had appeared—the Communists and the Socialists—and had been allowed to grow. Chile had a labor relations system highly subject to manipulation by the government, but at the same time a political outlet for worker mobilization that was —by Latin American standards—remarkably free. This creation of parallel outlets came later in Argentina. The labor relations structure emerging after 1943 was under the thumb of the executive, subsequently indistinguishable from the person of Perón. The political outlet for worker energy also soon became Perón's (and Evita's until her death in 1952) personal creature.

These political movements in Argentina and Chile, despite their differences, had one feature in common. Both survived the coups that removed the leaders they had supported. In Argentina as well as Chile, it was not enough for the military simply to remove a head of state they considered drifting into dangerous waters. In both cases military juntas—the Chilean in 1973 and the Argentine in 1955, 1966, and 1976— have faced a much larger task. They have had to struggle against well-established and institutionalized political movements based on urban worker support. In other words, the military's strategy of creating a highly controllable labor relations system proved inadequate for containing the political threat of the working class. Today, both military governments have regular recourse to extreme repression. Corporatist labor relations systems were not enough.

Brazil, by contrast, had never seen the establishment of major working-class political movements. The Communist Party (PCB), which enjoyed a brief surge in 1946 when it gained 10 percent of the presidential vote, was outlawed the following year.[69] Despite the law, the PCB was able to run candidates under other party labels, but its success in the years between 1947 and 1964 was negligible. A Socialist party of significance had never developed in Brazil, despite sporadic efforts by intellectuals in 1945–1946 and later. The closest approximation was the Partido Trabalhista Brasileiro (PTB), which Vargas founded in 1945 as an electoral vehicle to combine the growing urban working-class vote with certain traditional political machines (such as the one in his state of Rio Grande do Sul). Although by the early 1960s it was chosen by most militant leftist politicians as the best prospect within the established party spectrum, it remained very mixed, with a mildly reformist position characterizing the median opinion of its office holders. Thus the Brazilian military, when they seized power in 1964 and later deepened their hold by the further authoritarian turn in 1968, did not face a political problem of the same dimension as their Argentine counterparts had faced since 1955, and the Chilean officers were to face after 1973. Brazil had never developed the highly class-oriented politics of Peronist Argentina and post-1945 Chile. The Brazilian military could afford to rely on the corporatist labor relations system that their predecessor officers had made possible during the Estado Nôvo, since the extra-union political institutions attempting to represent urban workers in any militant manner were so insignificant.

How can we account for the similarities and differences in the three countries? How do we explain the varying fate of working-class organizers? the rise and fall of the Anarchists, the Anarcho-Syndicalists, and the Syndicalists? the varying fate of the Communists, the Socialists—a label with very different meanings in Argentina and Chile—the Trotskyists, and the reformists? the varying strength and resiliency of individual unions? the varying forms of labor and social welfare law? the variations in interpretation and application of those laws? What are the most likely explanatory factors?[70]

These questions are enough to occupy scholars for years. Satisfactory answers can come only from detailed knowledge of differing periods in each country. Nonetheless, it is important to think through the range of probable factors at work. A start toward comparison based on one indicator has been made by the recent research on labor law. Howard Wiarda, author of a number of works on corporatist systems in Iberia and Latin America, has given an overview of the principal legal codes governing labor in each Latin American country (and Spain and Portugal).[71] He finds a common corporatist orientation, although with more local variations than he had expected. Ruth and David Collier have added an important further step to that analysis by examining the mix of "inducements" and "constraints" in the major labor laws in each country.[72] They are thereby able to show—at least in law—how the dominant elites sought to proportion the carrot and the stick in dealing with labor. Although very valuable in guiding further research, these studies suffer from two serious limitations. First, both concentrate on those laws which explicitly focus on labor relations. This necessarily omits other laws which, while not mentioning labor per se, may have been equally important. An example would be the subversion or alien deportation laws. For obvious reasons they are an important part of the "constraints" on labor. Second, neither study gives attention to how the laws were applied. That, of course, is a huge task which these authors could hardly be expected to tackle and which will require monographic research on each case.

What follows is a listing and brief discussion of some of

the historical factors that may prove most worthy of investigation as research in Latin American labor history continues. There is no pretense at a systematic, comparative evaluation of these factors, even for the three countries covered in this essay. It is, rather, an exploratory discussion intended to draw together some of the themes which have emerged earlier.

## Significant Historical Factors

(1) *Foreign influences:* Just as we should not overestimate factors from abroad, as may have happened in studies of Argentine Anarchism, so they should not be underrated. Latin America produced few original thinkers in the field of class analysis, labor relations, industrial organizations, or social welfare. Latin Americans frankly and openly shopped for ideas abroad, especially in Europe. This was true not only of the elites, as when the Chileans Moisés Poblete Troncoso and Malaquías Concha Ortiz searched French, German, and British experience for useful precedents in labor and social welfare law, but also of the working-class organizers, as when Argentines and Brazilians eagerly sought the latest ideas of a visiting Elisée Réclus or a traveling Errico Malatesta. This dependence on foreign ideas and ideologies was not unique to the field of labor. It was part of Latin America's asymmetrical relationship with European and North American (more the former than the latter before 1914) culture. Indeed, irritation over and protest against this dependence intermittently clouded discussions of labor relations in all three countries discussed here. Nationalist critics charged both labor leaders and social welfare theorists with importing alien ideas, antithetical to the "true" traditions of Argentina, or Brazil, or Chile.

As we have seen in the case of Chile, it was not necessary to have a phalanx of European immigrants for Anarchist and Syndicalist ideas to take root and flourish. Ideas and doctrines had a life of their own. Yet the nature of the ideas that prevailed could in part be explained by the pattern of cultural affinities between Latin America and Europe. Spain and Italy, the two primary suppliers of immigrants to Latin

America, were strongholds of Anarchism. And Latin America's extreme Francophilic orientation in culture made French Syndicalism more important than the Democratic Socialism of Germany and Britain, two countries of lesser cultural influence.

The Versailles Treaty negotiations further intensified foreign influences on labor questions in Latin America. Part of the new post–World War I multilateral structure was a much-publicized International Labor Office, precursor of the International Labor Organization. Its creation gave Latin American countries such as Brazil, whose elite sought recognition for their country among the advanced nations of the world, the occasion to formulate labor codes and social welfare laws on "modern" lines. It was an institutionalization of the cultural dependence that had been more informal before 1914. For Latin American countries facing the "social question" these intellectual ties overseas were at least as important as the more obvious links of economic dependence via markets, investment, and loans.

(2) *Ideologies of working-class mobilization:* To what extent did ideologies—Anarchism, Syndicalism, Communism, reformism—gain adherents because their messages fit the circumstances and world outlook of the leaders and/or workers? To what extent did those ideologies, in turn, influence the shape of subsequent labor relations? To take an obvious example, why did Anarchism and Syndicalism fade so quickly, after having dominated the urban labor scene until the early 1920s? Was it because, as critics later charged, their ideology grew increasingly anachronistic, given the character of ongoing industrialization? Was it because their organizational structure made them especially vulnerable to government repression (as compared to the clandestine parallel structure the Communists later mounted)? Was it because their antipolitical emphasis—often seen by workers as utopian—roused the scepticism of the battle-weary followers? On the other hand, the Anarchists' antipolitical message must have fit well the experience of Brazilian or foreign-born Argentine workers, who were effectively excluded from the political system. And it should be remembered that the Anar-

chist leaders had also often proved capable, contrary to later historical interpretations, of leading well-disciplined, workplace-level strikes on bread-and-butter issues.

In a later era, when repression was the order of the day, the Communist expertise at surviving underground, in part due to the Party's extreme emphasis on discipline, made it especially "appropriate," in historical terms. It also carried the prestige of a victorious revolution in Russia, which gave Communist ideology the luster of European success, a virtue that Anarchism and Syndicalism notably lacked.

(3) *Cohesion of the dominant elites:* When the challenge from urban labor became acute, consensus among the ruling classes/sectors was put to the test. Of first importance was the nature of the political system. We have seen that Chile was the prime case of a society in which the middle-sector political leaders, epitomized by Alessandri, sought working-class electoral support. This was true to a lesser degree of Yrigoyen in Argentina; in Brazil there was no counterpart, largely because the Brazilian middle sectors had yet to gain a foothold in their struggle against the incumbent oligarchy.

Here we should note the consequences of Latin America's telescoped political experience. As we have seen, the question of labor relations arose as a major political issue at an early stage of industrialization. Political evolution analogous to that in Western Europe had not yet taken place. Most important, a reformist-oriented middle-sector political movement —like those of Alessandri and Yrigoyen in their more generously pro-labor moments—had not yet gained enough ground for it to be able to make partial common cause with the urban workers in a struggle against the traditional political powers. In all three countries the middle sectors proved susceptible to the appeals of reactionary leaders who warned them that they had much to lose in the social revolution that their concessions might encourage.

(4) *Prevailing elite conceptions of ideal labor relations:* This factor is closely linked to the cohesion of the dominant elites. Here we are concerned with the ideas—spelled out in legal proposals—of elite spokesmen as to how labor relations ought to be structured. We have seen that corporatist ideas

were important in Brazil and Chile. Argentina and Brazil both produced elite reasoning about labor similar to that in Chile; yet we lack studies comparable to that of James Morris on the Chilean case. Ample evidence for Brazil is available in the debates over the abortive proposals of maverick Congressman Maurício de Lacerda, who in 1919 introduced bills calling for social welfare legislation and a labor code.[73] There were similar initiatives and accompanying debates in Argentina. It appears that Latin American political elites adopted a common attitude toward urban labor: if it must be dealt with, then it should be within a carefully circumscribed legal web of obligations and regulations. But the exact similarities and differences in these stances in the three countries deserve more attention.

(5) *Economic conditions:* This rubric covers one of the most important and pervasive factors. Here we are asked to apply some of the fundamental questions of labor economics. What are the basic characteristics of the labor market? How is it defined? To what extent is there differentiation by skill? What is the supply/demand relationship by skill category? What are the wage differentials? To what extent are they correlated with verifiable job skills? What of the impact of immigration and internal migration on labor supply? All of these questions point to a key question about modern labor markets: are they segmented, i.e., not exhibiting the homogeneity that classical economics has posited?[74] This seemingly technical question leads directly to the vital issue of a "labor aristocracy," whose privileged economic status might create an unbridgeable gap between itself and the unskilled or less skilled. Equally important, have the privileged workers attained and preserved their position by exhibiting scarce skills, or by maintaining institutional barriers? A prime example would be the need for the job applicant to present work papers, which in turn could be obtained only after extraordinary effort (e.g., presenting a birth certificate—often difficult for many workers, whose parents may have been common-law partners at best). Such barriers, which in economic terms have nothing to do with the worker's productive capacity, are typical features of labor surplus economies. To identify barriers of

this type requires patient historical research; it has seldom yet been done for Latin America. Aside from artificial barriers, there is the need to evaluate the labor supply at historical junctures—a difficult task all too seldom attempted in Latin American labor history.[75]

There is also the question of the macroeconomic context. Labor relations are greatly influenced by the basic trend of the economy—if it is growing, then workers may have a relative advantage, since labor may be scarce. If strong demand exists, then firms can pass along increased labor costs in their prices. The result can be a favorable bargaining position for the workers. Rapid growth also produces *new* jobs, which in turn help transform the labor market.

A further macroeconomic factor is price behavior. We have seen that inflation has repeatedly caused great hardship for workers, whose wages invariably rise more slowly than prices. Workers have often been slow to understand the principle of real versus nominal wages; once learned, however, the lesson is a powerful incentive to militant action. Not infrequently, as we have seen, it has driven workers to aggressive strike action.

Finally, there is labor turnover. To what extent were workers able to gain job security? Were employers able to dismiss workers at will, thereby tapping the pool of the unemployed or underemployed? This brings us back to the basic question of the equilibrium between supply and demand for labor, at all the appropriate skill (wage differential?) levels. In the last analysis, these questions may be the most important in helping understand what happened to Latin American workers. As yet, we are left with inadequate data on these questions. Recent research indicates that better answers are there for the finding. It remains for serious students of Latin American labor history to probe the specifics of market conditions.

(6) *Worker consciousness:* To what extent was the attitude of workers a factor? How did they perceive the short-run and the long-run interests of labor? Did real democracy exist within the unions? Were workers in the more privileged industries prepared to sacrifice for the benefit of their com-

rades in less favored sectors? To what extent did the union leaders have to respond to initiatives from below?

These questions will require a great deal of future research. At this stage we can only guess at the answers and their relative importance. Nonetheless, tentative conclusions are in order.

## Conclusions

First, the political elites of Brazil and Chile have had little trouble in creating labor relations systems subject to elaborate government supervision. The model is corporatist, drawn from a mélange of influences prominent in the interwar period. These included Catholic corporatist ideas, as well as Fascist doctrines from Italy and Germany, although it should be noted that the first proposals to the Congress for a Chilean code predated Mussolini's march on Rome. In Argentina organized labor has proved more independent, although under Perón it was thoroughly subordinated to the government. In neither Brazil nor Chile was an authentic collective bargaining system, à la the U.S. or Western Europe, a live possibility. The elites of those two countries effectively eliminated that option, preferring a highly structured system that would avoid the unpredictability of a free market framework.

Second, we need to look more carefully at the nature of corporatism in Latin America. There is an irony in leftist labor leadership's attitude toward the corporatist systems of official labor relations in two of the three countries. The pattern is clearest in Chile. In the early 1920s the leftist leaders vigorously denounced the labor code proposals which were eventually merged in the 1924 code. For the following decade most continued to condemn this structure as a device to distort the authentic representation of workers' interests. By the mid-1930s, however, some leaders began to see how useful this structure could be if *they* (or their responsive political allies) reached power. With the formation of the Popular Front government in 1938 they got their opportunity. They were able to manipulate the corporatist machinery for what they regarded as the interests of the working class.[76] Thus even the most militant elements in the labor movement eventually allowed themselves to participate within the corporatist structure.

After 1947 the situation became more complicated. The ideological left wandered in the political wilderness (in terms of gaining governmental power). But it had the power to defend its hegemony within the labor union structure. An important test came in the presidency of Eduardo Frei (1964–1970), when the President's political party, the Christian Democrats, challenged the Communists and Socialists at the plant level, the crucial point of competition for union representation according to the 1924 code. The Christian Democrats wanted to amend the regulations, which stipulated that the union group with the largest vote won the right to represent all the workers of that plant. The Christian Democrats, usually running third in plant-level votes, proposed that any union with at least one-third of the vote should be included in the officially recognized union representation.[77] But the opposition to Frei controlled a majority in Congress and blocked any change in the corporatist-inspired system of union recognition. The Christian Democrats lost. Meanwhile, the leftist leadership of labor preserved its stronghold of control over union locals and bided its time for the next presidential election. The leftists' patience and tenacity were rewarded. With the election of Allende in 1970, as with the Popular Front government of 1938, the leadership of the ideological left, identified primarily with the Communist and Socialist parties, was able to use the extensive governmental labor relations apparatus and legal authority for its own ends. The Unidad Popular government had ambitious plans for revising the labor relations system.[78] But events moved too quickly. With the coup of 1973, this labor leadership felt the full force of its enemies' replacing the system with an instrument for maximum government control of workers.

The pattern in Brazil offered some similarities. The corporatist labor relations system was codified during the authoritarian Estado Nôvo (1937–1945), when labor leaders of the left were either in prison, in hiding, or in incubation. In 1945, however, that leadership suddenly burst on the scene. The

Communist Party enjoyed a brief surge of support, gaining an impressive foothold among urban workers in São Paulo. When the Party was outlawed in 1947, the Communist leadership in the labor movement suffered a purge, but they managed to re-emerge by the early 1950s. Thenceforth, the Communist labor leaders continuously debated the question of whether they should seek to compete for control of the unions within the extremely circumscribed boundaries of the corporatist structure. By the mid-1950s, the Communists had opted for the system. They met with growing success, reaching the height of their influence in 1962–1964. In those years they found a receptive President in João Goulart, who moved steadily left in his three years of office between 1961 and his ouster in 1964. Although the militant leftists, who included non-Communists as well as Communists, had not reached the degree of effectiveness achieved by their Chilean counterparts of the Allende era, they were beginning to benefit from their privileged access to the corporatist machinery of the official labor relations system.[79] Here, as in Chile, the military coup was a rude return to reality. Despite early comments about the need to "reform" the labor relations structure, the military-civilian regime taking power in 1964 quickly discovered the convenience of being able to manipulate the labor union system through the enormous powers of the Ministry of Labor. Unlike their Chilean counterparts, however, they did not have to revamp the machinery. The corporatist creations of an earlier era, intermittently capitalized upon by organized labor's left leadership, had become the all-too-efficient property of a repressive military regime.

Argentina never got as complete a corporatist straitjacket as Chile or Brazil. The Argentina military frequently intervened in the area of labor relations, often revising its legal structure. One of the first priorities of the Pedro Aramburu government (1955–1958) was a thorough overhaul of the Ley de Asociaciones Profesionales. The subsequent military regimes have intermittently attempted to create a labor relations system more responsive to government command. They have been frustrated by an organized labor movement far more self-sufficient and used to autonomous decision-making than the Brazilian counterpart. The comparison with Chile raises more difficulties, however. Why has the Argentine labor movement been able to preserve more bargaining power under repressive military regimes than the Chileans? One answer might be that the Chilean regime has been far more ruthless in its treatment of the labor movement. For reasons whose elucidation would necessarily go beyond the limits of this essay, the Argentine military leaders in the 1970s have not been able to match the explicitly anti-labor posture of their Chilean colleagues. As a result, labor unions in Argentina have been able to preserve greater identity and legitimacy than either their Brazilian or their Chilean counterparts.

What does this brief historical inquiry tell us about contemporary Latin America? First, we can see more clearly the great importance of the years before 1930. It was an era when dramatic class confrontations left a strong impression on both ruling elites and demonstrating workers. The great general strikes of 1917–1920 (and later in Chile) frightened the politicians and employers. Their multiple responses, running from paternalistic social welfare legislation to police repression, set the framework for the labor relations systems of our own day. A deeper appreciation of this historical process has been lost behind the prevailing historical wisdom about passive masses, shrewdly manipulative elites, and the "self-defeating" tactics of Anarchists and Syndicalists. Historians have underrated the mass mobilizations of urban workers, expressed in militant strikes. This wave of large-scale mobilizations belies the standard picture of ruling classes little concerned before 1945 with the great potential of their masses. The ideas, styles, and institutions on which the elites relied in the Great Depression were spelled out in the critical years during World War I and shortly thereafter.

Despite the sustained efforts of the political elites, and especially of the military, in none of the three countries has the "social question" been resolved in the broader sense in which that phrase was used during the first two decades of the century. Worker participation in the structure of labor relations—deciding on such bread-and-butter issues as wages, working conditions, and work rules—has been denied and/or distorted. This is a dangerous legacy for economies in which industry and relatively sophisticated service sectors will be important in future economic development. The improvement of productivity, for example, will depend upon more meaningful employee participation than corporatist structures now allow. In part this is the psychological dimension of the "social question" as it was debated decades ago. The operation of a modern capitalist industrial economy requires a minimum of consensus, of shared values. In England, France, and the United States that was achieved within a pluralistic political system, where competing social sectors came to acknowledge each other as legitimate contenders for material benefits and status recognition.[80] In the early 1970s Argentina, Brazil, and Chile became garrison states, in which the highly unequal distribution of benefits could be maintained only by military power: the soldier versus the worker. The technological expertise of the military, combined with the weight of political socialization in these highly patrimonial societies, continues to favor the men in uniform. To a surprising degree, however, the moment of confrontation seems similar to those dramatic years during and just after the first Great War, when fiery Anarchist and Syndicalist organizers summoned urban workers to challenge the ruling elites.

# Notes

## Popular Challenges and Elite Responses: An Introduction

1. Richard Graham, *Britain and the Onset of Modernization in Brazil, 1850–1914*, Cambridge Latin American Studies, 4 (Cambridge, Eng.: Cambridge University Press, 1968).
2. See pp. 40 and 79.
3. P. 43.
4. P. 45.
5. P. 107.
6. P. 47.

## Cultures in Conflict: The Implication of Modernization in Nineteenth-Century Latin America

1. Fernando Uricoechea, *Intelectuales y desarrollo en América latina* (Buenos Aires: Centro Editor de América Latina, 1969), pp. 40–42.
2. For a general and useful introduction to the roles intellectuals play in new nations, see John Friedman, "Intellectuals in Developing Societies," *Kylos: International Review for Social Sciences*, 13, Fasc. 4 (1960): 513–544.
3. Carlos Medinaceli, *La inactualidad de Alcides Argüedas y otros estudios biográficos* (La Paz: Los Amigos del Libro, 1972), pp. 93–94.
4. Quoted in José Luis Romero, *A History of Argentine Political Thought* (Stanford: Stanford University Press, 1963), p. 145.
5. Medinaceli, *La inactualidad*, p. 144.
6. José Enrique Rodó wrote in 1903 that Facundo exerted a profound influence in all of Latin America (*La tradición intelectual argentina* [Buenos Aires: Editorial Universitaria de Buenos Aires, 1968], pp. 16–17).
7. Pedro Calmón, *História de D. Pedro II* (Rio de Janeiro: José Olympio, 1975), 1:405–406.
8. D. F. Sarmiento, *Life in the Argentine Republic in the Days of the*

*Tyrants; or, Civilization and Barbarism* (New York: Hafner, n.d.), p. 42.

9. Atilio García Mellid, *Montoneras y caudillos en la historia argentina* (Buenos Aires: Editorial Universitaria de Buenos Aires, 1974), p. 42. The government's policy was to eradicate the Indians (Ramón Tissera, "Cuando gobernar era despopular," *Todo Es Historia* [Buenos Aires], no. 96 [May 1975]: 56, 58). Such genocide extended to the gaucho as well. Sarmiento wrote to Bartolomé Mitre: "Do not try to save gaucho blood. It is the fertilizer needed to make our nation flourish. Blood is the only thing the gaucho has which is human" (cited in Manuel Gálvez, *Vida de Sarmiento* [Buenos Aires, 1952], p. 245). While still associated with the Generation of 1837, Juan Bautista Alberdi pronounced, "In order to civilize by means of populations, it is necessary to do it with civilized people; in order to educate our America in liberty and industry it is necessary to populate it with the peoples of Europe most advanced in liberty and industry as happens in the United States" (*Bases y puntos de partida para la organización política de la República Argentina* [Buenos Aires: La Cultura Argentina, 1916], pp. 14–15; first edition, 1852).

10. Solomon Lipp, *Three Chilean Thinkers* (Waterloo, Ontario, Canada: Wilfrid Laurier University Press, 1975), p. 16. For Bilbao's discussion of the people of the countryside, see *Sociabilidad chilena*, reprinted in *Obras completas de Francisco Bilbao* (Santiago: Imprenta de Buenos Aires, 1865), 1:28–30, passim.

11. For a fascinating analysis of *Amalia*, see the perceptive essay by Hernán Vidal, "*Amalia*: Melodrama y Dependencia," *I & L: Ideologies & Literature*, 1, no. 2 (February–April 1977): 41–69.

12. Clorinda Matto de Turner, *Aves sin nido* (Buenos Aires: Solar/ Hachette, 1968), p. 38.

13. Ibid., pp. 15–16.

14. Ibid., p. 19.

15. Ibid., p. 167.

16. Ibid., p. 120.

17. Ibid., p. 131.

18. In another essay, also published in 1889, Matto de Turner further emphasized the importance of education as a solution to the debasement of the Indians. In order to educate the people, Peru needed "more free schools, industries, factories, work, and honor among men" (quoted in Francisco Carillo, *Clorinda Matto de Turner y su indigenismo* [Lima: Ediciones de la Biblioteca Universitaria, 1967], p. 33). A few years later, in 1904, Manuel González Prada wrote in quite a different vein that only the Indians could redeem themselves, and the first step would be rebellion. "Every white man is more or less a Pizarro" (*Horas de lucha* [Lima: Ediciones Peisa, 1969], p. 235).

19. Euclides da Cunha, *Rebellion in the Backlands* (Chicago: University of Chicago Press, 1957), pp. 464, 78.

20. Ibid., p. 481.
21. Da Cunha found an intellectual ally in his respect for the people of the interior in the aristocrat Eduardo Prado, who noted, "The *caboclo* is a man whom all of us must admire for his energy and because, when all is said, it is he who is Brazil, the real Brazil, very different from the artificial cosmopolitanism in which we, the inhabitants of this great city, live. It was he who made Brazil" (quoted by Thomas E. Skidmore, "Eduardo Prado: A Conservative Nationalist Critic of the Early Brazilian Republic, 1889–1901," *Luso Brazilian Review*, 12, no. 2 [Winter 1975]: 155).
22. Da Cunha, *Rebellion*, pp. 408, 454.
23. A renowned twentieth-century Mexican intellectual, Octavio Paz, practically paraphrased da Cunha when he observed, "The Third World is *condemned* to modernity and the task confronting us is not so much to escape this fate as to discover a less inhuman form of conversion" (quoted in *Time*, January 29, 1973, p. 85).
24. Jorge Moreal, "Americanismo," *Dom Quixote* (Rio de Janeiro), 1, no. 8 (1895): 3. In an interesting parallel with Argentina, these descriptions duplicate Sarmiento's characterization of the Indian, African, and Spaniard (*Life in the Argentine Republic*, p. 11).
25. The attitudes toward the bleaching process are summarized by Thomas E. Skidmore, *Black into White: Race and Nationality in Brazilian Thought* (New York: Oxford University Press, 1974), pp. 64–69.
26. Magnus Morner, *Race Mixture in the History of Latin America* (Boston: Little, Brown and Company, 1967), pp. 104–105.
27. In this paragraph to this point, I have drawn heavily from the useful essay by T. G. Powell, "Mexican Intellectuals and the Indian Question, 1876–1911," *Hispanic American Historical Review*, 48, no. 1 (February 1968): 37–58.
28. The literature on modernization in general and on modernization in Latin America in particular is vast. Some of the widely recognized and quoted studies are: Marion J. Levy, *Modernization and the Structure of Societies: A Setting for International Affairs*, 2 vols. (Princeton: Princeton University Press, 1966); Cyril Black, *The Dynamics of Modernization: A Study in Comparative History* (New York: Harper & Row, 1967); S. N. Eisenstadt, *Modernization: Protest and Change* (Englewood Cliffs, N.J.: Prentice-Hall, 1966); I. R. Sinai, *In Search of the Modern World* (New York: American Library, 1967); David E. Apter, *The Politics of Modernization* (Chicago: University of Chicago Press, 1967); and Joseph A. Kahl, *The Measurement of Modernism: A Study of Values in Brazil and Mexico* (Austin: University of Texas Press, 1968). Another useful work is Peter Berger, Brigitte Berger, and Hansfried Kellner, *The Homeless Mind: Modernization and Consciousness* (New York: Vintage, 1974). I agree with these authors in their equation for the Third World of modernization with Westernization (p. 131) and with their conclusion that modernization de-cultures

the Third World, creating "a spreading condition of homelessness" (p. 138). I admire the critique of modernization made by Dean C. Tipps, "Modernization Theory and the Comparative Study of Societies: A Critical Perspective," *Comparative Studies in Society and History*, 15, no. 2 (March 1973): 119–226. He notes that the concept of modernization is popular because it obscures rather than clarifies (p. 199) and that ethnocentric criteria becloud modernization theories (p. 206). There are three excellent studies of the modernization process in nineteenth-century Latin America: Richard Graham, *Britain and the Onset of Modernization in Brazil, 1850–1914* (Cambridge, Eng.: Cambridge University Press, 1968); Roberto Cortés Conde, *The First Stages of Modernization in Spanish America* (New York: Harper & Row, 1974); and Edward Dennis Hernández, "Modernization and Dependency in Costa Rica during the Decade of the 1880s" (Ph.D. dissertation, University of California, Los Angeles, 1975).

29.    Col. Alvaro Gabriel Barros, *Actualidad financiera de la República Argentina* (Buenos Aires: Imp. Librerías de Mayo, 1875), quoted in *La Opinión Cultural* (Buenos Aires), June 7, 1975, p. 2.

30.    Fermin Chávez, *Civilización y barbarie en la historia de cultura argentina* (Buenos Aires: Ediciones Theoría, 1974), p. 56.

31.    Juan Bautista Alberdi, *Obras completas* (Buenos Aires: Imprenta de la Tribuna Nacional, 1887), 4: 69.

32.    Ibid., 7: 156; see also Alberdi's *Escritos postumos* (Buenos Aires: Imprenta Europa, 1848), 10: 241.

33.    *Obras completas*, 4: 68.

34.    Ibid., 7: 166.

35.    Ibid., 7: 163–164.

36.    "To civilize ourselves, to improve ourselves, to perfect ourselves according to our needs and our means: that is our national destiny which can be summarized by this single word: Progress" (quoted in José Ingenieros, *La evolución de las ideas argentinas* [Buenos Aires: El Ateneo, 1951], 2: 499).

37.    José Hernández, *The Gaucho Martín Fierro* (Albany, N.Y.: State University of New York Press, 1974), p. 83.

38.    Alberto J. Pla, *Ideología y método en la historiografía argentina* (Buenos Aires: Ediciones Nueva Visión, 1972), p. 42.

39.    "Indeed, much capital for development in the first half of the nineteenth century came from local merchants themselves. The arrival of modern industrial technology in the latter half of the century sustained Argentine economic expansion but cost creoles their control of domestic processing and transport. Although modern technology made possible new exports of beef and wheat, it proved expensive. . . . Argentine merchants lost much of their previous command of the commercial infrastructure. 'Neocolonialism' and 'dependency'—if they ever characterized economic development in Argentina—certainly postdate 1860. In the first half of the nineteenth century, the

economy of the Río de la Plata had responded to foreign trade in a way that expanded the locally dominated marketing and processing system at Buenos Aires" (Jonathan C. Brown, "Dynamic and Autonomy of a Traditional Marketing System: Buenos Aires, 1810–1860," *Hispanic American Historical Review*, 56, 4 [November 1976]: 629).

40. For Hernández's view on the question of land reform, see his essay, "La división de la tierra," published in *El Río de la Plata* (Buenos Aires), September 1, 1879.

41. Sílvio Romero, *História da literatura brasileira*, 2d ed. (Rio de Janeiro: H. Garnier, 1902), 1: 11.

42. Ibid., 1: 102.

43. João Capistrano de Abreu, "O caracter nacional e as origens do povo brasileiro," *O Globo* (Rio de Janeiro), March 9, 1876, p. 3.

44. João Capistrano de Abreu, *Ensaios e estudos* (Rio de Janeiro: Briguiet, 1931), 1: iii.

45. Germán Carrera Damas has made an excellent summary and analysis of this book in his *Temas de historia social y de las ideas* (Caracas: Ediciones de la Biblioteca de la Universidad Central de Venezuela, 1969), pp. 139–165.

46. Ramón Ramírez, *El cristianismo y la libertad: Ensayo sobre la civilización americana* (Caracas: Imprenta de V. Espinal, 1855), p. xii.

47. Ignacio Manuel Altamirano, *Christmas in the Mountains* (Gainesville: University of Florida Press, 1961), pp. 6–7, 66.

48. Quoted by Joaquín V. González, "Estudio Preliminar," in *Mis montañas* (Buenos Aires: Editorial Kapelusz, 1965), p. xix.

49. I expand on this idea in "Ideology in Nineteenth-Century Latin American Historiography," *Hispanic American Historical Review*, 58, no. 3 (August 1978): 409–431.

50. Robert K. Merton, "The Sociology of Knowledge," *Isis*, no. 75, vol. 27, no. 3 (November 1937): 493; Edward Hallett Carr, *What Is History?* (New York: Random House, 1961), p. 42; Gunnar Myrdal, *Objectivity in Social Research* (London: Gerald Duckworth, 1970), p. 44; Felix Gilbert, "Intellectual History: Its Aims and Methods," *Daedalus*, 100, no. 1 (Winter 1971): 87–88; Norman Pollack, "Fear of Man: Populism, Authoritarianism, and the Historian," *Agricultural History*, 39, no. 2 (April 1965): 60–64.

51. Ricardo Levene, *Las ideas históricas de Mitre* (Buenos Aires: Casa Editora Coni, 1948), p. 87.

52. Pla, *Ideología*, p. 33.

53. Bartolomé Mitre, *Correspondencia literaria, histórica, y política del General Bartolomé Mitre* (Buenos Aires: Coni Hermanos, 1912), 3: 284.

54. Romero, *History of Argentine Political Thought*, pp. 82, 89.

55. Although these paragraphs reflect some influence of Robert Redfield, "The Folk Society," *American Journal of Sociology*, 52, no. 4 (January 1947): 293–308, and Gideon Sjoberg, "Folk and 'Feudal' Societies,"

*American Journal of Sociology,* 58, no. 3 (November 1952): 231–239, I feel most indebted to the ideas of George M. Foster, "What is Folk Culture?" *American Anthropologist,* 55, no. 2, part 1 (April–June 1953): 159–173. Foster's concept of "folk culture" harmonizes with and has influenced my own interpretations of the popular alternatives in nineteenth-century Latin America.

56. Robert E. Gamer, *The Developing Nations: A Comparative Perspective* (Boston: Allyn and Bacon, 1976), pp. 61–62, 97–98.

57. Roberto Ares Pons, "Sed de padres," *La Opinión* (Buenos Aires), April 27, 1975, p. 9.

58. Romero, *History of Argentine Political Thought,* pp. 124, 127.

59. Juan Bautista Alberdi, *Grandes y pequeños hombres del Plata,* 4th ed. (Buenos Aires: Editorial Plus Ultra, 1974), pp. 154, 161, 155.

60. Manuel Gálvez, "Vida de Aparicio Saravia," in *Biografías completas de Manuel Gálvez* (Buenos Aires: Emecé Editores, 1962), p. 1540. The first edition was published in 1942.

61. Arturo Jauretche, *Política nacional y revisionismo histórico* (Buenos Aires: Editorial A. Peña Lillo, 1959), p. 61.

62. Rodolfo Ortega Peña and Eduardo Luis Duhalde suggest how popular songs of the 1860s can be used to revise the standard historical view of that period in *Folklore argentino y revisionismo histórico* (Buenos Aires: Editorial Sudestada, 1967).

63. Leonardo Paso, *Los caudillos: Historia o folklore* (Buenos Aires: Silaba, 1969), p. 190.

64. Popular culture as a form of resistance to elitist domination is the subject of a provocative essay by Luigi M. Lombardi Satriani, "Folklore y cultura popular," *Los Libros* (Buenos Aires, January–February, 1975), pp. 3–9; Paso, *Los Caudillos: Historia o Folklore,* p. 190.

65. Paulo de Carvalho-Neto, *El folklore de las luchas sociales* (Mexico City: Siglo Veintiuno Editores, 1973), p. 155.

66. Emilio F. Moran, "Some Semantic Categories in Brazilian Caboclo Folk Narratives," *Luso-Brazilian Review,* 11, no. 2 (Winter 1974): 221.

67. Merle E. Simmons, *The Mexican Corrido as a Source for Interpretive Study of Modern Mexico (1870–1950)* (Bloomington: Indiana University Press, 1957), pp. 7, 33.

68. Ibid., p. 35; Mark J. Curran, "A página editorial do poeta popular," *Revista Brasileira de Folclore,* no. 32 (January–April 1972): 5.

69. Sjoberg, "Folk and 'Feudal' Societies," p. 234.

70. Dr. Pedro Molina expressed this idea well in a public speech, September 16, 1832, Guatemala City, reprinted in Hector Humberto Samayoa Guevara, *La enseñanza de la historia en Guatemala (desde 1832 hasta 1852)* (Guatemala City: Imprenta Universitaria, 1959), pp. 113–120.

71. Ralph Lee Woodward, Jr., *Social Revolution in Guatemala: The Carrera Revolt,* Middle American Research Institute Publication 23, no. 3 (New Orleans: Tulane University, 1971), p. 50.

72. Rafael Carrera understood that function of the Church and discussed it sympathetically in his *Informe que dirijió el Presidente de la República de Guatemala al Cuerpo Representativo, en su instalación el día 15 de Agosto de 1848* (Guatemala City: Imprenta de la Paz, 1848), p. 3.

73. Ignacio Solis, ed., *Memorias del General Carrera, 1837–1840* (Guatemala City: Tipografía Sánchez & De Guise, 1906), p. 15.

74. Carrera, *Informe* . . . *1848*, p. 3.

75. Ibid., pp. 2–3.

76. *El Noticioso* (Guatemala City), October 26, 1861.

77. The revised view of the Carrera period needs further testing and support. Keith L. Miceli offers a useful revisionist perspective in "Rafael Carrera: Defender and Promoter of Peasant Interests in Guatemala," *The Americas*, 31, no. 1 (July 1974): 72–95. In his recent *Central America: A Nation Divided* (New York: Oxford University Press, 1976) Ralph Lee Woodward, Jr., takes a cautiously revisionist stand on Carrera and well represents what Carrera signified for the Indian population. See particularly pp. 118–119. For a fuller consideration of this topic by Woodward, see his *Social Revolution in Guatemala*, pp. 63–64, 67, 68. Perhaps the earliest and one of the best revisionist studies in English is Max Leon Moorhead, "Rafael Carrera of Guatemala: His Life and Times" (Ph.D. dissertation, University of California, Berkeley, 1942). For the Guatemalan side of this revisionism, see particularly Manuel Coronado Aguilar, *Apuntes histórico-guatemalenses* (Guatemala City: Editorial José de Pineda Ibarra, 1975).

78. Manuel Coronado Aguilar, *El General Rafael Carrera ante la historia* (Guatemala City: La Editorial de Ejército, 1965), pp. 54–55.

79. Moorhead, "Rafael Carrera," pp. 62, 67; Woodward, *Social Revolution in Guatemala*, p. 68.

80. Woodward, *Social Revolution in Guatemala*, pp. 64, 68.

81. Ibid., p. 67.

82. *El Tiempo* (Guatemala City), August 30, 1839.

83. S. A. Lazard, "El Excelentísimo Señor Gral. Don Rafael Carrera," *El Progreso Nacional* (Guatemala City), May 7, 1895. Although unsympathetic to Carrera, this essay comments on his "frequent excursions to the departments." For an 1845 visit to Esquipulas, see Archivo General de Centro America, Guatemala City (abbreviated hereafter as AGCA), B119.2, Exp. 58175, Leg. 2535, Fol. 1 (December 20, 1845).

84. Information on the tax changes will be found in Woodward, *Social Revolution in Guatemala*, p. 63; *El Tiempo* (Guatemala City), February 25, 1840; and Miceli, "Rafael Carrera," pp. 78–79, 90–95.

85. Rafael Carrera, *Informe dirijido por el Exmo Sr. Presidente de la República de Guatemala Capitán General Don Rafael Carrera a la Cámara de Representantes en la Opertura de sus Segundas Sesiones, El día 25 de noviembre de 1853* (Guatemala City: Imprenta de la Paz, 1853), pp. 7–8.

86.    Sotero Carrera, *Bando de policía y buen gobierno expedido para el Departamento de Sacatepequez por su Corregidor y Comandante General Brigadier Sr. Sotero Carrera* (Guatemala City: Imprenta de la Aurora, 1849), AGCA Impreso No. 5096C.

87.    Coronado Aguilar, *El General Rafael Carrera*, 37; Woodward, *Social Revolution in Guatemala*, p. 68. Examples of the government's concern with communal lands can be found in the AGCA. See: B100.1, Expt. 33282, Leg. 1419 (April 12, 1841); B100.1, Exp. 33274, Leg. 1419 (November 29, 1841); B100.1, 33305, Leg. 1419 (November 14, 1843); B100.1, Exp. 33356, Leg. 1419 (November 2, 1844); B100.1, Exp. 5370, Leg. 3633 (March 15, 1853); and B100.1, Exp. 33326, Leg. 1419 (April 19, 1863).

88.    Moorhead, "Rafael Carrera," pp. 52, 120.

89.    Carrera, *Informe . . . 1848*, pp. 3, 9–10.

90.    "El antagonismo de razas," *El Noticioso* (Guatemala City), September 26, 1862.

91.    Miguel Boada y Balmes, "Fantasía," *El Noticioso* (Guatemala City), October 17, 1862.

92.    *El Noticioso* (Guatemala City), October 19 and December 11, 1861; see in particular the editorial in *La Semana* (Guatemala City), January 18, 1865.

93.    Carrera, *Informe . . . 1848*, p. 12.

94.    Felipe de Jesús, *María: Historia de una mártir*, 2d ed. (Guatemala City: Editorial José de Pineda Ibarra, 1967), pp. 27–30.

95.    Ibid., p. 175.

96.    David J. McCreery, "Coffee and Class: The Structure of Development in Liberal Guatemala," *Hispanic American Historical Review*, 56, no. 3 (August 1976): 444; Valentín Solórzano F., *Evolución económica de Guatemala*, Seminario de Integración Social de Guatemala Publicación No. 28 (Guatemala City: Editorial José de Pineda Ibarra, 1970), p. 350.

97.    Ibid., pp. 354, 356, 373–374.

98.    McCreery, "Coffee and Class," pp. 456–458.

99.    Oliver La Farge, "Maya Ethnology: The Sequence of Cultures," in *The Maya and Their Neighbors* (New York: Appleton-Century, 1962), p. 291. Alfonso Villa Rojas extends that conclusion to the Chiapas highlands in "The Concepts of Space and Time among the Contemporary Maya," in *Time and Reality in the Thought of the Maya*, ed. Miguel León Portilla (Boston: Beacon Press, 1973), p. 117. A similar effect of the Peruvian sugar industry on the Andean Indians in the late nineteenth century has been discussed by Jean Piel, "The Place of the Peasantry in the National Life of Peru in the Nineteenth Century," *Past and Present*, no. 46 (February 1970): 127, 131; and by Peter F. Klaren, *Modernization, Dislocation, and Aprismo: Origins of the Peruvian Aprista Party, 1870–1932* (Austin: University of Texas Press, 1973), pp. 26–31.

100. José A. Beteta, *Edmundo* (Guatemala City: Tipografía Nacional, 1896), pp. 23–24.

101. Evelyn Hu-Dehart, "Development and Rural Rebellion: Pacification of the Yaquis in the Late Porfiriato," *Hispanic American Historical Review*, 54, no. 1 (February 1974): 72–93.

102. Gary H. Gossen, "Translating Cuscat's War: Understanding Maya Oral History," *Journal of Latin American Lore*, 3, no. 2 (Winter 1977): 273.

103. Jean A. Meyer, *Problemas campesinos y revueltas agrarias (1821–1910)* (Mexico City: Sepsetentas, 1973), pp. 8–25, 66–67; John M. Hart, *Anarchism and the Mexican Working Class, 1860–1931* (Austin: University of Texas Press, 1978), pp. 62, 68–69, 78ff.

104. Nelson Reed, *The Caste War of Yucatán* (Stanford: Stanford University Press, 1964), p. 61.

105. Ibid., p. 220.

106. Victoria Reifler Bricker, "The Caste War of Yucatán: The History of a Myth and the Myth of History," in *Anthropology and History in Yucatán*, ed. Grant D. Jones (Austin: University of Texas Press, 1977), pp. 256–257.

107. Oswaldo Albornoz P., *Las luchas indígenas en el Ecuador* (Guayaquil: Editorial Claridad, n.d.), pp. 33–50.

108. Robert Brent Toplin, "Upheaval, Violence and the Abolition of Slavery in Brazil," *Hispanic American Historical Review*, 49, no. 4 (November 1969): 646.

109. Prince Adalbert, *Travels in the South of Europe and in Brazil* (London, 1849), 2: 43–44.

110. Two scholars who devote attention to slave resistance in nineteenth-century Latin America are Leslie B. Rout, Jr., *The African Experience in Spanish America: 1502 to the Present* (Cambridge, Eng.: Cambridge University Press, 1976), pp. 185–312; and Emília Viotti da Costa, *Da senzala à colonia* (São Paulo: Difusão Européia do Livro, 1966), pp. 305–329.

111. For an excellent study of this novel as well as others germane to this topic, see Raymond S. Sayers, *The Negro in Brazilian Literature* (New York: Hispanic Institute, 1956).

112. João José Reis, "A elite baiana face os movimentos sociais, Bahia: 1824–1840," *Revista de História* (São Paulo), 54, no. 108, year 27 (1976): 341–348.

113. Manuel Correia de Andrade, "The Social and Ethnic Significance of the War of the Cabanos," in *Protest and Resistance in Angola and Brazil: Comparative Studies*, ed. Ronald H. Chilcote (Berkeley and Los Angeles: University of California Press, 1972), p. 103.

114. Hélio Vianna, *História do Brasil* (São Paulo: Edições Melhoramentos, 1961), 2: 118.

115. Quoted in Roderick J. Barman, "The Brazilian Peasantry Reexamined: The Implications of the Quebra-Quilo Revolt, 1874–1875," *Hispanic*

American Historical Review, 57, no. 3 (August 1977): 402, 409. For another new interpretation of the Quebra-Quilo Revolt, see Geraldo Irinêo Joffily, "O Quebra-Quilo (A revolta dos matutos contra os doutores) (1874)," Revista de História (São Paulo), 54, no. 107, year 27 (1976): 69–145.

116. Barman offers an excellent summation of the significance of the Quebra-Quilo Revolt: "As this essay has attempted to demonstrate, the peasants in the agreste possessed a well-established independent culture and social system. They were neither on the margin of society, nor were the goals of the revolt unrealistic. The peasants achieved precisely what they intended. Indeed the Quebra-Quilo revolt can be classed as an unusually successful and sophisticated example of a form of action—the riot—commonly employed in preindustrial and premodern societies by groups outside the official world to call attention to their views and needs and to block official activities which they considered detrimental to their interests. Since such forms of action did not aim at taking control of or giving positive direction to the body politic, they can be described as prepolitical. Whether or not this lack of 'political consciousness' is to be deplored, it should not be equated with a lack of comprehension or with an inability to act efficiently, as the Quebra-Quilo revolt demonstrates" ("The Brazilian Peasantry Reexamined," p. 423).

117. José Nicolás Matienzo, El gobierno representativo federal en la República Argentina (Madrid: Editorial America, 1910), p. 130.

118. Quoted by J. León Helguera, "Antecedentes sociales de la Revolución de 1851 en el Sur de Colombia (1848–1849)," Anuario Colombiano de Historia Social y de la Cultura (Bogotá), no. 5 (1970): 55.

119. "Railroads, Landholding, and Agrarian Protest in the Early Porfiriato," Hispanic American Historical Review, 54, no. 1 (February 1974): 49ff.

120. Ezequiel Gallo, Farmers in Revolt: The Revolutions of 1893 in the Province of Santa Fé, Argentina (London: Athlone Press, 1976).

121. E. J. Hobsbawm, Primitive Rebels: Studies in Archaic Forms of Social Movement in the 19th and 20th Centuries (New York: W. W. Norton, 1965). Bryan R. Wilson makes a useful connection between revolution and millennialism which is applicable to the Latin American experience in Magic and Millennium: A Sociological Study of Religious Movements of Protest among Tribal and Third-World Peoples (New York: Harper & Row, 1973), p. 196.

122. Maria Isaura Pereira de Queiroz, Images messianiques du Brésil (Cuernavaca, Mexico: Centro Intercultural de Documentación, 1972), Sondeos No. 87, p. 3/21. A different interpretation of the messianic movements will be found in René Ribeiro, "Brazilian Messianic Movements," in Millennial Dreams in Action: Essays in Comparative Studies, ed. Sylvia L. Thrupp, Comparative Studies in Society and History, Supplement II (The Hague: Mouton, 1962), pp. 55–69. Ralph Della Cava carries the interpretations of Pereira de Queiroz one step

further: "The purpose of this paper is to demonstrate that the popular religious movements at Canudos and Joaseiro were from the outset not isolated from, but rather were intimately tied into the national ecclesiastical and political power structures of imperial and republican Brazil; and that they were also enmeshed within a changing nationwide economy" ("Brazilian Messianism and National Institutions: A Reappraisal of Canudos and Joaseiro," *Hispanic American Historical Review*, 48, no. 3 [August 1968]: 404). A summary and a useful analysis of the messianic movements in Brazil will be found in Maria Isaura Pereira de Queiroz, "Messiahs in Brazil," *Past and Present*, no. 31 (July 1965): 62–86.

123. Pereira de Queiroz, *Images messianiques*, p. 2/5.

124. Shepard Forman, *The Brazilian Peasantry* (New York: Columbia University Press, 1975), pp. 237–240.

125. Sue Anderson Gross suggests the complexity of motivation of Brazilian bandits in "Religious Sectarianism in the Sertão of Northeast Brazil, 1815–1866," *Journal of Inter-American Studies*, 10, no. 3 (July 1968): 372; while Maria Isaura Pereira de Queiroz summarizes the activity of bandits in nineteenth-century Brazil in *Os Cangaceiros: Les Bandits d'honneur brésiliens*, Collection Archives No. 34 (Paris: Julliard, 1968), pp. 52–72. For Mexico, John M. Hart suggests a link between banditry and agrarian revolutionaries: "Predictably, areas that previously produced social banditry—Chalco, Río Frío, eastern Morelos, and northwestern Puebla—now produced heavily agrarian revolutionaries" (*Anarchism and the Mexican Working Class*, p. 62).

126. Pereira de Queiroz, *Os Cangaceiros*, p. 196; Eric J. Hobsbawm, *Bandits* (New York: Dell, 1969), p. 13.

127. Manoel Calvalcanti Proenca, ed., *Literatura popular em verso* (Rio de Janeiro: Casa de Rui Barbosa, 1964), 1: 322–343.

128. Piel, "The Place of the Peasantry," p. 130.

129. Enrique López Albujar, *Los caballeros del delito: Estudio criminológico del bandolerismo en algunos departamentos del Peru* (Lima: Compañía de Impresiones y Publicidad, 1936), p. 40.

130. Ibid., p. 184.

131. Ignacio Manuel Altamirano, *El Zarco, the Bandit* (London: Folio Society, 1957), pp. 103–104.

132. Ibid., p. 58.

133. D. Bouquet y Soler, "Recuerdos de Copan-Calé," *El Noticioso* (Guatemala City), August 1 and 18, September 2, 6, and 23, 1862.

134. However, Maria Isaura Pereira de Queiroz has drawn some convincing conclusions from her many studies of messianic movements in Brazil. See her "Messiahs in Brazil," pp. 62–86.

135. Information in the following paragraphs is based on the current revision of nineteenth-century Paraguayan history. I am particularly indebted to: Richard Alan White, *Paraguay's Autonomous Revolution, 1810–1840* (Albuquerque: University of New Mexico Press, 1978);

León Pomer, *La guerra del Paraguay: Gran negócio* (Buenos Aires: Ediciones Caldén, 1968); Atilio García Mellid, *Proceso a los falsificadores de la historia del Paraguay* (Buenos Aires: Ediciones Theoría, vol. 1, 1963; vol. 2, 1964); Carlos Pastore, *La lucha por la tierra en el Paraguay* (Montevideo: Editorial Antequera, 1972); Teresa Zárate, "Parcelación y distribución de las tierras fiscales en el Paraguay (1870−1904)," *Revista Paraguaya de Sociología*, 10, no. 26 (January−April 1973): 121−140; John Hoyt Williams, "Paraguay's 19th Century Estancias de la República," *Agricultural History*, 47, no. 3 (July 1975): 206−216; John Hoyt Williams, "Foreign Técnicos and the Modernization of Paraguay, 1840−1870," *Journal of Interamerican Studies and World Affairs*, 19, no. 2 (May 1977): 233−257; Thomas Lyle Williams, "The Iron Works of Ibycui: Paraguayan Industrial Development in the Mid-Nineteenth Century," *The Americas*, 35, no. 2 (October 1978): 201−218.

136. Robin W. Winks, "On Decolonization and Informal Empire," *American Historical Review*, 81, no. 3 (June 1976): 543.

137. Cortés Conde, *The First Stages of Modernization in Spanish America*, pp. 66ff.

138. Hernández, "Modernization and Dependency in Costa Rica."

139. Although most studies credit Latin America with economic growth in the nineteenth century, there is evidence that such growth was sporadic rather than consistent. Eric R. Wolf points to declining absolute and per capita agricultural production in Mexico during the last quarter of the century, while prices rose and wages remained constant (*Peasant Wars of the Twentieth Century* [New York: Harper & Row, 1969] p. 19). William Paul McGreevey indicates a "reversal in the slow growth of Colombia's economy" in *An Economic History of Colombia, 1845−1930* (Cambridge, Eng.: Cambridge University Press, 1971), p. 146. Nathaniel H. Leff has questioned the conclusion long posited by Celso Furtado and others that Brazil experienced a remarkable economic growth in the nineteenth century, particularly during the last half. Instead, Leff notes "Brazil's slow aggregate growth during most of the nineteenth century" in "A Technique for Estimating Income Trends from Currency Data and an Application to Nineteenth-Century Brazil," *Review of Income and Wealth*, ser. 18, no. 4 (December 1972): 365.

140. Morner, *Race Mixture in the History of Latin America*, p. 106. Speaking of the nineteenth century, Morner observes, "The same age that witnessed the high bourgeoisie's rise and prosperity in Latin America also witnessed deterioration in the living conditions of the working masses, most of them people of darker skin."

141. Charles C. Cumberland, *Mexico: The Struggle for Modernity* (New York: Oxford University Press, 1968), p. 204.

142. Ibid., p. 232.

143. Meyer, *Problemas campesinos*, pp. 222−223.

144. Powell, "Mexican Intellectuals and the Indian Question," p. 19. "It is common knowledge among students of Mexican history," says Powell, "that during the era of Porfirio Díaz (1876–1911) the misery of the nation's large Indian population increased substantially." Friedrich Katz states that "Of the many profound transformations which took place in the Mexican countryside in the period between 1876 and 1910, two have been emphasized: the expropriation of the lands of communal villages, and the decrease in real wages paid to laborers on haciendas. By the end of the Porfiriato over 96 percent of the communal villages had lost their lands, according to available data. The buying power of wages paid to agricultural laborers on haciendas sharply declined between 1876 and 1910" ("Labor Conditions on Haciendas in Porfirian Mexico: Some Trends and Tendencies," *Hispanic American Historical Review*, 54, no. 1 [February 1974]: 1).

145. Wolf, *Peasant Wars*, pp. 19–20. Wolf points out that, "despite the growth of the latifundium, agricultural production as a whole did not grow steadily and consistently. From 1877 to 1894, in fact, agricultural production declined at an annual rate of 0.81 percent. From 1894 to 1907, it rose once more, but only at a slow annual rate of 2.59 percent. The upward trend was due in major part to the growth of industrial crops for consumption within the country and even more to the growth of export crops. . . . But food crops declined steadily. This was especially true of the production of maize, the staple food of the population. Per capita production of maize declined from 282 kilograms in 1877 to 154 in 1894, to 144 in 1907. Similar declines are noted for beans and chile, similarly vital food crops. Not only did the amount of maize produced per capita decline, but corn prices rose, while wages remained stationary. All indications are that the average daily wage had not increased between the beginning of the nineteenth century and 1908." Rodney D. Anderson, *Outcasts in Their Own Land: Mexican Industrial Workers, 1906–1911* (DeKalb, Ill.: Northern Illinois University Press, 1976), p. 63, points out the "spectacular" rise of food prices at the turn of the century in Mexico. He provides some grim examples: "In the Federal District the price of *frijoles* (beans) rose from 2.95 pesos a kilo in 1899 to 10.89 pesos in 1908. More importantly for the workers' budget, corn rose from 2.19 pesos per kilo in 1887 to 6.40 in 1908. From 1900 to 1908 the wholesale price of corn rose as follows: Mexico (the state), 30 percent; Puebla, 45 percent; Jalisco, 56 percent; Veracruz, 65 percent. Corn was the most important single expense for most Mexicans, save perhaps rent, and its increasing price was a disaster."

146. Cumberland, *Mexico*, p. 204. Meyer, *Problemas campesinos*, p. 33, also contends that the rural workers were worse off at the end of the nineteenth century than they had been at the beginning.

147. Aldo Ferrer, *The Argentine Economy: An Economic History of Argentina* (Berkeley and Los Angeles: University of California Press,

1967), p. 117. Discussing the decades 1860–1930, Ferrer concludes that, for the Argentine workers, "Rural wages went up less than the depreciation of the currency and the rise in agricultural and livestock prices, so that profit margins of rural entrepreneurs increased while the share of agricultural workers in the income of this sector declined." Carl Solberg points out that whole regions and social classes were excluded from the export boom of the last half of the nineteenth century. He maintains that "The vast bulk of farm workers received wages that were totally insufficient to maintain a decent year-round standard of living. During the late nineteenth century, real wages of rural workers declined seriously, as the classic work of economist John H. Williams demonstrates" ("Farm Workers and the Myth of Export-Led Development in Argentina," *The Americas*, 31, no. 2 [October 1974]: 121ff., 134).

148. Ibid., p. 138.
149. For specific information on the deteriorating condition of rural workers in Tucumán, including the quotations from *La Razón*, consult Manuel García Soriano, "La condición social del trabajador en Tucumán durante el Siglo XIX," *Revisión Histórica* (Tucumán), 1, no. 1 (May 1960): 7–46.
150. McCreery, "Coffee and Class," pp. 456–458.
151. Arnold J. Bauer, "Chilean Rural Labor in the Nineteenth Century," *American Historical Review*, 76, no. 4 (October 1971): 1074, 1076, 1083.
152. Arnold J. Bauer, *Chilean Rural Society from the Spanish Conquest to 1930* (Cambridge, Eng.: Cambridge University Press, 1975), pp. 159–160. Prior to 1890, Bauer finds that real wages stayed constant, except that they may have declined slightly toward 1890.
153. Nathaniel H. Leff, "Tropical Trade and Development in the Nineteenth Century: The Brazilian Experience," *Journal of Political Economy*, 81, no. 3 (May–June 1973): 691. See also Leff, "A Technique for Estimating Income Trends from Currency Data and an Application to Nineteenth Century Brazil," pp. 361, 362.
154. Peter L. Eisenberg, *The Sugar Industry in Pernambuco, 1840–1910: Modernization without Change* (Berkeley and Los Angeles: University of California Press, 1974), pp. 60, 219. Eisenberg notes that "At the same time basic food prices of manioc flour, beans, and jerked beef rose, with the result that real income fell even faster than wages" (p. 231). Celso Furtado concurs that per capita income declined in the Northeast. See *The Economic Growth of Brazil: A Survey from Colonial to Modern Times* (Berkeley and Los Angeles: University of California Press, 1963), p. 158.
155. Eisenberg, *Sugar Industry in Pernambuco*, p. 214.
156. McGreevey, *Economic History of Colombia*, p. 145.
157. Ibid., p. 180.
158. Cumberland, *Mexico*, p. 224.

159. James R. Scobie, *Buenos Aires: Plaza to Suburb (1870−1910)* (New York: Oxford University Press, 1974), pp. 137−140, 266, 268.
160. Ibid., pp. 140−141.
161. Ferrer, *The Argentine Economy*, p. 118.
162. Eulália M. L. Lobo, "Evolution des prix et du coût de la vie à Rio de Janeiro (1820−1930)," in *L'Histoire quantitatif du Brésil de 1800 à 1930*, Colloques Internationaux du Centre Nacional de la Recherche Scientifique, No. 543 (Paris: Centre Nacional de la Recherche Scientifique, 1971), pp. 211−212. For a similar discussion of the declining real wages of urban workers see Lobo, *História do Rio de Janeiro (Do capital comercial ao capital industrial e financeiro)* (Rio de Janeiro: IBMEC, 1978), 1: 232ff. Generalizing about the growing Brazilian cities of the nineteenth century, Gilberto Freyre speaks of "more poverty, more suffering" (*The Mansions and the Shanties: The Making of Modern Brazil* [New York: Knopf, 1963], p. 24). Richard M. Morse offers for consideration the suggestion that export-oriented and dependent economies negatively shaped nineteenth-century urbanization in Latin America ("Export-Led Growth and Urban Change in Latin America," *Annals of the Southeastern Conference on Latin American Studies*, 5 [March 1974]: 56−65).
163. Rodney D. Anderson's study of Mexican industrial labor provides an excellent example. He indicates that Mexican workers spent over 60 percent of their earnings on food and another 17 percent on rent. Their diet was probably insufficient. Prices during the last decade of the century rose, while salaries stagnated: "The overwhelming conclusion is that the wages of most industrial workers in Mexico were barely sufficient to meet their minimum needs. This was especially true after 1900, and perhaps before. In the textile town of Orizaba one writer for a local newspaper noted in 1893 that as factories were established in the town, misery accompanied them. 'There is poverty, great poverty, and the struggle for living is becoming increasingly difficult . . . and today life in Orizaba is painful (but not so for those who have capital). In addition to this, the cost of living increases daily, and labor is compensated disgracefully'" (*Outcasts in Their Own Land*, pp. 63−66).

## Workers and Soldiers: Urban Labor Movements and Elite Responses in Twentieth-Century Latin America

1. Many of the ideas for this paper arose out of a seminar on twentieth-century Latin American labor movements which I have offered at the University of Wisconsin in recent years. I am grateful to the students in those seminars, and especially to Peter DeShazo, who helped plan one seminar and who was generous with his knowledge of the Argentine and Chilean cases. I am indebted also to Eugene Sofer, Rolando

Mellafe, John Coatsworth, Simon Collier, and Alan Angell for very helpful comments, and to Richard Graham for his commentary on the version of this paper presented as part of the B. K. Smith Lectures at the University of St. Thomas in 1978. I received many valuable comments on a subsequent draft from fellow participants in a Workshop on Urban Working Class Culture and Social Protest in Latin America at the Latin American Program of the Woodrow Wilson International Center for Scholars (Washington, D.C.) in late 1978. I am grateful to Lou Goodman, David Montgomery, Henry Landsberger, Gianfranco Pasquino, and especially Ruth Collier and J. Samuel Valenzuela. Hobart Spalding, Kenneth Erickson, Paulo Sergio Pinheiro, Solomon Levine, and Richard U. Miller offered valuable bibliographical help. The final product is, alas, my responsibility. It is a pleasure to acknowledge the warm hospitality of Professors Ann Q. Tiller and Virginia Bernhard of the Department of History, as well as other officials of the University of St. Thomas, on the occasion of the delivery of the original version of this paper. Financial support has come from the Graduate School Research Committee and the Cyril Nave Fund, both at the University of Wisconsin.

2. This point is acknowledged in Adolf Sturmthal, *Comparative Labor Movements: Ideological Roots and Institutional Development* (Belmont, Calif.: Wadsworth, 1972).

3. Bruce H. Millen, *The Political Role of Labor in Developing Countries* (Washington, D.C.: Brookings Institution, 1963); Sidney Sufrin, *Unions in Emerging Societies* (Syracuse, N.Y.: Syracuse University Press, 1964); Clark Kerr, John T. Dunlop, Frederick Harbison, and Charles Myers, *Industrialism and Industrial Man* (Cambridge, Mass.: Harvard University Press, 1960); Walter Galenson, ed., *Labor and Economic Development* (New York: John Wiley, 1959). More sensitivity to the Latin American experience is shown in Everett M. Kassalow, "Unions in New and Developing Countries," in *National Labor Movements in the Postwar World*, ed. Kassalow (Evanston, Ill.: Northwestern University Press, 1963), pp. 225–253.

4. See, for example, Clinton Bourdon, "Craft Unions and the Organization of Work in Construction," *European Studies Newsletter* (Council for European Studies, Columbia University), 7, no. 2 (November/December 1977): 1–11; 7, no. 3 (February 1978): 1–5. For a very useful synthesis and historiographical overview on unionization in Britain from the late Victorian era to 1933, see John Lovell, *British Trade Unions, 1875–1933* (London: Macmillan, 1977).

5. The most influential single work in this direction has been E. P. Thompson, *The Making of the English Working Class* (New York: Alfred A. Knopf, 1963). A leading example of the new approach in the U.S. and one which also discusses historiographical trends, is Herbert G. Gutman, "Work, Culture, and Society in Industrializing America,

1815–1919," *American Historical Review*, 78, no. 3 (June 1973): 531–588.

6.  Important questions about the frequent resort to such concepts as "modernization" and "tradition" have been raised by Daniel T. Rodgers, "Tradition, Modernity, and the American Industrial Worker: Reflections and Critique," *Journal of Interdisciplinary History*, 7, no. 4 (Spring 1977): 655–681. For an example of a relatively uncritical application of the "modernization" model to Latin America, see Wilbert Moore, *Industrialization and Labor* (Ithaca, 1951), which includes a case study of Mexico.

7.  This point is discussed cogently in Eugene F. Sofer, "Recent Trends in Latin American Labor Historiography: A Review Essay," forthcoming in the *Latin American Research Review*.

8.  Given the difficulty of keeping straight the ideological orientation of leaders and movements during this era in Latin America, it is reassuring to hear from a specialist on Europe that "anyone who has tried to write about anarchism sometimes comes to a point at which he wonders just what it is he is writing about." The observation is from James Joll's review of Jean Maitron's two-volume history of French anarchism in the *Times Literary Supplement*, September 10, 1976. Joll suggests that even Maitron, "who has devoted a lifetime to the subject, seems to have had much the same experience."

9.  For a passionate defense of the post-Stalinist attempt by continental scholars to rediscover the full range of labor history, especially in its international dimension, see Georges Haupt, "Why the History of the Working-Class Movement?" *Review*, 2, no. 1 (Summer 1978): 5–24.

10. For a comprehensive survey of this important question, see Glen G. Cain, "The Challenge of Segmented Labor Market Theories to Orthodox Theory," *Journal of Economic Literature* (December 1976): 1215–1257.

11. For an example, see Subbiah Kannappan, ed., *Studies of Urban Labour Market Behavior in Developing Areas* (Geneva: Institute for International Labour Studies, 1977), which includes an excellent bibliography. For a wide-ranging discussion of the varying circumstances surrounding the emergence of labor markets, see Bert F. Hoselitz, "The Development of a Labor Market in the Process of Economic Growth," in *The International Labor Movement in Transition*, ed. Adolf Sturmthal and James G. Scoville (Urbana: University of Illinois Press, 1973), pp. 34–57.

12. Alexander conducted his doctoral dissertation research in Chile in 1946–1947, and in succeeding years he traveled widely in Latin America, interviewing many of the leading figures in labor unions and left-wing political movements. He drew on these first-hand sources in his many publications. Alexander was always forthright about his ideological assumptions, as in the final chapter of *Communism in Latin*

*America* (New Brunswick, N.J.: Rutgers University Press, 1957), which was entitled "The Right and the Wrong Way to Fight Communism in Latin America."

13. The most valuable recent overview of Latin American labor history is Hobart A. Spalding, Jr., *Organized Labor in Latin America: Historical Case Studies of Urban Workers in Dependent Societies* (New York: Harper & Row, 1977). Spalding's synthesis offers an excellent point of departure for further research, and his footnotes provide an up-to-date bibliography of the field. Partly for that reason I shall not attempt any extensive review of the historiography of the country cases. For an important earlier inventory of interpretations and sources, see Kenneth Paul Erickson, Patrick V. Peppe, and Hobart Spalding, Jr., "Research on the Urban Working Class and Organized Labor in Argentina, Brazil, and Chile: What is Left to be Done?" *Latin American Research Review*, 9, no. 2 (Summer 1974): 115–142. For further examples of recently suggested interpretive schema, see note 35 below.

14. Two papers from the Pátzcuaro conference are especially relevant for the study of organized union labor: Barry Carr, "The Casa del Obrero Mundial, Constitutionalism and the Pact of February 1915," and Aurelio de los Reyes, "Historiografía," the latter being an overview of the principal historical interpretations; some of de los Reyes's critical evaluations seem exaggerated. Labor in Mexico has been a subject of much recently published research, to which Chapter 3 of Spalding, *Organized Labor in Latin America*, is a ready guide. Among the most significant recent titles are Rodney D. Anderson, *Outcasts in Their Own Land: Mexican Industrial Workers, 1906–1911* (DeKalb: Northern Illinois Press, 1976); Rámon Eduardo Ruiz, *Labor and the Ambivalent Revolutionaries: Mexico, 1911–1923* (Baltimore: Johns Hopkins University Press; Barry Carr, *El movimiento obrero y la política en México, 1910–1929*, 2 vols. (Mexico City, 1976); José Luis Reyna et al., *Tres estudios sobre el movimiento obrero en México* (Mexico City, 1976); and *La formación del proletariado industrial en México*, which occupies all of *Revista Mexicana de Ciencias Políticas y Sociales*, n.s. 21, no. 83 (January–March 1976).

15. A colloquium on "Sindicalismo en América Latina," sponsored by CLACSO, was held in Buenos Aires in 1972, and the papers were published in *Temas de economía laboral: movimiento obrero, sindicatos y poder en América Latina* (Buenos Aires: Editorial El Coloquio, 1974) (organized by the Centro de Estudios e Investigaciones Laborales [CEIL] de la Facultad de Ciencias Económicas de la Universidad Nacional de la Plata). The CLACSO group has had a number of subsequent meetings and seminars and is preparing further publications.

16. The trend can be noted, for example, in the research grants awarded at both the doctoral dissertation and postdoctoral level by the SSRC-

ACLS Joint Committee on Latin American Studies: Social Science Research Council, *Annual Report: 1975–76; Annual Report: 1976–77* (New York).

17. A representative issue is vol. 3, no. 1 (Winter 1976), entitled *Imperialism and the Working Class in Latin America.*

18. Further proof of this interest is the publication in English of an edited version of Guillermo Lora's first-hand analysis of Bolivia: *A History of the Bolivian Labour Movement* (Cambridge, Eng.: Cambridge University Press, 1977). The condensation of Lora's several volumes is by Laurence Whitehead, and the translation is by Christine Whitehead.

19. An obvious exception is the group of French scholars associated with *Sociologie du Travail*, which has published a number of articles on Latin American labor movements, especially in Brazil. See, for example, Alain Touraine and Daniel Pécaut, "Conscience ouvrière et développement économique en Amérique Latine: Propositions pour une recherche," *Sociologie du Travail*, 9, no. 3 (July–September 1967): 229–254. Scholarship in the U.S.S.R. and Eastern Europe has also produced studies of Latin American labor movements and working-class history, but they have received little notice in the West, in part because of lack of knowledge of Slavic languages among Western Latin Americanists, in part because of the heavy-handed and dogmatic approach so often typical of historical scholarship in those countries, and in part because they offer no research originality, since the authors can almost never, for obvious reasons, gain access to primary sources. For an analysis of one labor-related theme in Soviet writings on Latin American history in the years between 1957 and 1964, see Edward B. Richards, "Marxism and Marxist Movements in Latin America in Recent Soviet Historical Writing," *Hispanic American Historical Review*, 44, no. 4 (November 1965): 577–590.

20. For a recent study of events in Europe, see Albert S. Lindemann, *The "Red Years": European Socialism versus Bolshevism, 1919–1921* (Berkeley: University of California Press, 1974), which focuses on the socialist parties in France, Italy, and Germany. Recent studies of Anarchism and Syndicalism in Europe include Jean Maitron, *Le Mouvement anarchiste en France*, 2 vols. (Paris: F. Maspero, 1975), and Bob Holton, *British Syndicalism, 1900–1914: Myths and Realities* (London: Pluto Press, 1976).

21. A typical example is Hernán Ramírez Necochea, *Origen y formación del Partido Communista de Chile* (Santiago: Talleros Gráficos Santaro, 1965), who begins his discussion of Anarchism (p. 20) thus: "Los anarquistas, por lo general individuos de extracción artesanal o pequeñoburguesa, con su prédica llena de attractivos conceptos revolucionarios, fijaban falsos objectivos y erróneos métodos a las luchas proletarias." The most reliable survey of the history of Latin American Communist Parties is Boris Goldenberg, *Kommunismus in*

*Lateinamerika* (Stuttgart: Verlag W. Kohlhammer, 1971), which includes chapters on all the major countries.

22. Representative is the treatment in Jacques Lambert, *Latin America: Social Structure and Political Institutions* (Berkeley: University of California Press, 1967), pp. 190–199. In order to document his claim that politicizing of unions has jeopardized bread-and-butter gains, Lambert is forced to give a misleading capsule account of Argentina in the last half of the 1950s. A much more careful examination of "political" versus "economic" orientation of labor is given in Henry A. Landsberger, "The Labor Elite: Is It Revolutionary?" in *Elites in Latin America*, ed. Seymour Martin Lipset and Aldo Solari (New York: Oxford University Press, 1967), pp. 256–300. Landsberger argues that labor's political strength is, more often than not, greater than the strength deriving from its economic base. Landsberger correctly points out that many of the most important decisions affecting labor in post-1945 Latin America have been in the hands of the government, not the employers; ergo, the logic of workers seeking to put pressure directly on the government (political action), thereby bypassing the employers (economic action). The emphasis on politicization in Latin American labor relations is given its most extreme formulation in James L. Payne, *Labor and Politics in Peru: The System of Political Bargaining* (New Haven: Yale University Press, 1965). An extensive and enlightening discussion of the relationships among union members, union leaders, and political parties in Chile occupies a large part of Alan Angell's *Politics and the Labour Movement in Chile* (Oxford: Oxford University Press, 1972).

23. It should be noted that leaders and groups which sought to follow a more radical "political" line have been repeatedly driven out of the major U.S. labor unions. The massive struggle by the CIO after 1945 to capture control of the electrical workers from the dominant leadership (which included Communists) was a notable example. Revisionist interpretations are now challenging the standard versions of U.S. labor history, as in Jeremy Brecher, *Strike!* (San Francisco: Straight Arrow Press, 1972), which emphasizes the militancy of ordinary workers; and Stanley Aronowitz, *False Promises: The Shaping of American Working Class Consciousness* (New York: McGraw-Hill, 1973), which investigates "why the working class in America remains a dependent force in society."

24. It is sobering to recall the conclusions drawn from research on the relationship in the history of the industrialized countries between unionization and real wages or labor's share of the national income. These researchers have not found evidence that unions made any difference. The dynamic factor was growing productivity. See E. H. Phelps Brown and Margaret H. Browne, *A Century of Pay: The Course of Pay and Production in France, Germany, Sweden, the United*

*Kingdom, and the United States of America, 1860–1960* (London: Macmillan, 1968) and F. Ray Marshall, Allan M. Cartter, and Allan G. King, *Labor Economics*, 3d ed. (Homewood, Ill.: Irwin, 1976), p. 385. This is not to say, however, that unions have not had an effect on the distribution of income within labor's share (although there is disagreement on those effects) or on nonwage issues. For a brief but suggestive discussion of factors affecting the sectoral allocation of labor in Latin American economies, see Joseph R. Ramos, *Labor and Development in Latin America* (New York: Institute of Latin American Studies, Columbia University Press, 1970), pp. 174–180.

25.    Robert Alexander, a pioneer scholar in the study of Latin American labor, worked closely with the Free Trade Union Committee of the American Federation of Labor, and with Serafino Romualdi (long-time official of the Organización Regional Inter-Americana de Trabajadores [ORIT], the anti-Communist and anti-Peronist regional labor confederation strongly supported by the AFL), to whom Alexander dedicated his *Labor Relations in Argentina, Brazil, and Chile* (New York: McGraw-Hill, 1962). U.S. efforts to influence Latin American labor are roundly attacked in Spalding, *Organized Labor in Latin America*, Chapter 6. For Argentina there is *NACLA's Latin America and Empire Report*, 8, no. 9 (November 1974), entitled *Argentina: AIFLD Losing Its Grip*. For a critical view of the U.S. efforts when the Alliance for Progress was still young, see Frank Bonilla, "The Urban Worker," in *Continuity and Change in Latin America*, ed. John J. Johnson (Stanford: Stanford University Press, 1964), pp. 204–205. Adolf Sturmthal, one of the best-known students of comparative labor movements, in a recent paper refers to Anglo-Americans as exhibiting, in the postwar world, "a naïve belief in the universal applicability of some form of collective bargaining as the fundamental method of settling industrial relations problems." Yet the author spends the remainder of his paper analyzing why the collective bargaining model has not appeared—or appeared only in modified or scattered form— elsewhere and what forces might create it in the future! (Sturmthal, "Industrial Relations Strategies," in *The International Labor Movement*, ed. Sturmthal and Scoville, pp. 1–33.) Spalding's very useful survey seldom discusses Soviet penetration of Latin American labor unions and the manner in which Communists, especially in the Stalinist era, had to subordinate their analysis of their countries' economic and political situation to the dictates of Moscow.

26.    The horror of the 1973 coup in Chile has taken time to sink in among foreign—and many Chilean—observers of the Chilean scene. That country had seemed so successful at generating a wide consensus on the rules of the political game—Salvador Allende's accession to power was justifiably cited as proof of the maturity of the Chilean political system and public. Unfortunately, the consensus rapidly eroded after

1970. For radical views of that process, see *Latin American Perspectives*, 1, no. 2 (Summer 1974), entitled *Chile: Blood on the Peaceful Road*. An interpretation from a centrist position is to be found in Paul E. Sigmund, *The Overthrow of Allende and the Politics of Chile, 1964–1976* (Pittsburgh: University of Pittsburgh Press, 1977).

27. The success with which Peronism outlasted a series of military regimes is yet to be explained in a systematic manner. Among the useful analyses are Daniel James, "Power and Politics in Peronist Trade Unions," *Journal of Inter-American Studies and World Affairs*, 20, no. 1 (February 1978): 1–36, and the same author's "The Peronist Left, 1955–1975," *Journal of Latin American Studies*, 8, Part 2 (November 1976): 273–296. Sebastião C. Velasco e Cruz, "Estado, sindicato e instabilidade política: Argentina, 1955– 1970," *Dados*, no. 15 (1977): 43–59, stresses the extent to which the Peronist unions were able to preserve a degree of autonomy in this era. The recurrent stabilization attempts, and the worker resistance they generated, are analyzed skillfully in Gary W. Wynia, *Argentina in the Postwar Era: Politics and Economic Policy Making in a Divided Society* (Albuquerque: University of New Mexico Press, forthcoming).

28. The most detailed analysis of the 1968 strike movement is Francisco Weffort, "Participação e conflito industrial: Contagem e Osasco, 1968" Cadernos CEBRAP, 5 (São Paulo, 1972). Some observers argue that in recent decades organized urban labor in Brazil has greatly increased its consciousness and can be controlled only by extreme coercion from the government. Such is the view in Angela Mendes de Almeida and Michael Lowy, "Union Structure and Labor Organization in the Recent History of Brazil," *Latin American Perspectives*, 3, no. 1 (Winter 1976): 98–119, where the labor protest movement of 1967–1968 is given as proof of labor's very organizable discontent. For a first-hand account of the 1968 labor actions, see the interview with José Ibrahim, a leader of the Metallurgical Workers in Osasco, in *Veja*, no. 501 (April 12, 1978).

29. A systematic study of the operation of this system in the greater São Paulo region may be found in Kenneth S. Mericle, "Conflict Regulation in the Brazilian Industrial Relations System" (Ph.D. dissertation, University of Wisconsin, 1974), partially summarized in Mericle, "Corporatist Control of the Working Class: Authoritarian Brazil since 1964," in *Authoritarianism and Corporatism in Latin America*, ed. James M. Malloy (Pittsburgh: University of Pittsburgh Press, 1977), pp. 303–339.

30. One of the earliest systematic critiques of the predominant assumptions among U.S. Latin Americanists was Susanne J. Bodenheimer, *The Ideology of Developmentalism: The American Paradigm-Surrogate for Latin American Studies*, Sage Professional Papers in Comparative Politics, vol. 2 (Beverly Hills, Calif.: Sage Publications,

1971). For an analysis of how U.S. Latin Americanists' assumptions have shifted in recent years, see Abraham Lowenthal, "North American Perspectives on Comparative Latin American Studies and on Inter-American Relations: Some Informal Notes," in *Perspectives para o desenvolvimento dos estudos comparativos latino-americanos e relações internacionais*, ed. Bernardo Sorj and Maria Regina Soares de Lima (Rio de Janeiro, forthcoming), which updates the analysis presented in Lowenthal's "United States Policy toward Latin America: 'Liberal,' 'Radical,' and 'Bureaucratic' Perspectives," *Latin American Research Review*, 8, no. 3 (Fall 1973): 3–25.

31. The details are given in *Covert Action in Chile, 1963–73: Staff Report of the Select Committee to Study Governmental Operations with Respect to Intelligence Activities, United States Senate* (Washington, D.C., 1975). For an attempt to paper over the CIA's role in Chile, see David Atlee Phillips, *The Night Watch: Twenty-Five Years of Peculiar Service* (New York: Atheneum, 1977), pp. 236–255. His denials are unconvincing.

32. Indicative of this trend was the appearance of *Marxist Perspectives*, a new quarterly which made its debut in early 1978. Names on the editorial board and among the organizational secretaries indicate widely distributed support in the U.S. academic community. Issue no. 4 (Winter 1978) of the first volume includes John Womack, Jr.'s "The Mexican Economy during the Revolution, 1910–1920: Historiography and Analysis," in which there is a brief discussion of the literature on labor for that decade.

33. For a suggestive discussion of the manner in which researchers' political beliefs are related to the growth of interest in labor history, see E. J. Hobsbawm, "Labor History and Ideology," *Journal of Social History*, 7, no. 4 (Summer 1974): 371–381.

34. This point is made evident in Peter Flynn, "European Perspectives on European-Latin American Relations and Comparative Latin American Studies," in *Perspectives para o desenvolvimento*, ed. Sorj and Soares de Lima.

35. J. Samuel Valenzuela, "A Conceptual Framework for the Analysis of Labor Movement Development," paper prepared for the Workshop on Urban Working Class Culture and Social Protest in Latin America at the Latin American Program of the Woodrow Wilson International Center for Scholars (Washington, D.C.), November 30–December 1, 1978; Ruth Berins Collier and David Collier, "Inducements versus Constraints: Disaggregating 'Corporatism,'" forthcoming in the *American Political Science Review*; and Elizabeth Jelin, "Orientaciones e ideologías obreras en América Latina," *Estudios Sociales*, no. 3 (Buenos Aires: Centro de Estudios de Estado y Sociedad, 1976). For examples of earlier secondary surveys that were unsatisfactory in part because of the lack of monographic literature, see Robert J. Alexander,

*Organized Labor in Latin America* (New York: Free Press, 1965) and Victor Alba, *Politics and the Labor Movement in Latin America* (Stanford: Stanford University Press, 1968).

36. In the latest edition of a leading textbook on labor economics (Marshall, Cartter, and King, *Labor Economics*) the authors argue vigorously for the use of the comparative method and devote five chapters to varying patterns of unionization, although in fact they include little *explicit* comparison. A strong appeal for the comparative approach to Latin America is made in John Womack, Jr., "Mexican Political Historiography, 1959–69," in *Investigaciones contemporáneas sobre historia de México: Memorias de la Tercera Reunión de Historiadores Mexicanos y Norteamericanos* (Mexico City, 1971), p. 486, where Womack laments the continuing provincialism among historians specializing in Mexico. His criticism applies equally well to specialists on Argentina, Brazil, and Chile. Too few have attempted well-documented comparative analysis of differing country cases within Latin America. An example of how effectively this approach can be employed is Elisabeth Jelin, "Spontanéité et organisation dans le mouvement ouvrier: Le Cas de l'Argentine, du Brésil et du Mexique," *Sociologie du Travail*, 18 (1976): 139–168.

37. I have argued this point for the cases of Argentina, Brazil, and Mexico in "The Politics of Economic Stabilization in Postwar Latin America," in *Authoritarianism and Corporatism in Latin America*, ed. Malloy, pp. 149–190.

38. I do not mean to suggest that labor protest and elite response can alone explain the pattern and dynamics of authoritarian government in the Latin America of the 1960s and 1970s. Such an explanation requires a broad-ranging analysis of many factors, including the relationship between the structure of political systems and the character of economic development in the last several decades. The most innovative and influential attempt in this direction has been by Guillermo O'Donnell, whose latest formulation is "Reflections on the Patterns of Change in the Bureaucratic-Authoritarian State," *Latin American Research Review*, 13, no. 1 (1978): 3–38. His work has been discussed in David Collier, "Industrial Modernization and Political Change: A Latin American Perspective," *World Politics*, 30, no. 4 (July 1978): 593–614, and is an essential point of reference in the forthcoming *The New Authoritarianism in Latin America*, edited by Collier (to be published by the University of California Press). My aim here is to isolate one factor—the confrontation of government and organized workers—and explore its historical roots.

39. A painstakingly annotated bibliography on this period can be found in Roberto Cortés Conde and Stanley J. Stein, eds., *Latin America: A Guide to Economic History, 1830–1930* (Berkeley: University of California Press, 1977), which includes chapters on Argentina (Tulio Hal-

perín Donghi), Brazil (Nícia Villela Luz), and Chile (Carmen Cariola and Osvaldo Sunkel). For Chile, the most complete analysis of this period is to be found in Markos J. Mamalakis, *The Growth and Structure of the Chilean Economy* (New Haven: Yale University Press, 1976). For Brazil, there is Wilson Cano, *Raízes da concentração industrial em São Paulo* (São Paulo, 1977). For Argentina, the basic work remains Carlos F. Díaz Alejandro, *Essays on the Economic History of the Argentine Republic* (New Haven: Yale University Press, 1970). Roberto Borges Martins, in his "Crescimento exportador, desigualdade e diversificação econômica: Uma comparação entre o Brasil e a República Argentina, 1860–1930," *Cadernos do Departamento de Ciência Política* (Faculdade de Filosofia e Ciências Humanas, Universidade Federal de Minas Gerais), no. 3 (March 1976): 55–106, clarifies the important differences in the degree of economic development of the two countries over this period, with Argentina's structure approximating that of the industrial economies of the North Atlantic, while Brazil retained a much larger rural subsistence sector.

40. A useful starting point for comparative analysis of the major South American labor relations systems is Alexander, *Labor Relations in Argentina, Brazil, and Chile.*

41. The classic statement on surplus labor in developing societies was W. Arthur Lewis, "Economic Development with Unlimited Supplies of Labour," *The Manchester School of Economic and Social Studies,* 22, no. 2 (May 1954): 139–191. For a refutation, based on Latin American data, see Richard U. Miller, "The Relevance of Surplus Labour Theory to the Urban Labour Markets of Latin America," *International Institute for Labour Studies Bulletin,* 8 (1971): 220–245.

42. Adolf Sturmthal, "Industrial Relations Strategies," in *The International Labor Movement,* ed. Sturmthal and Scoville.

43. On the rent strike, see Hobart Spalding, *La clase trabajadora argentina: Documentos para su historia—1890–1912* (Buenos Aires: Editorial Galerna, 1970), pp. 447–496.

44. In the brief historical sketches that follow I have attempted to give the outlines of the essential trends in each country, with emphasis on the historical precedents established in both class relationships and legal structures. Unfortunately, the secondary sources are often contradictory on matters of fact; as a result, I offer these sketches as strictly tentative portraits.

45. Much of my analysis of Argentine labor mobilization is drawn from Peter DeShazo, "The Failure of Revolutionary Labor Syndicates in Argentina, 1900–1930," (unpublished paper, University of Wisconsin, History Department, October 1973), and from Richard Alan Yoast, "The Development of Argentine Anarchism: A Socio-Ideological Analysis," (Ph.D. dissertation, University of Wisconsin, 1975).

46.    Immigrant labor leadership figures prominently in Carl Solberg, *Immigration and Nationalism: Argentina and Chile, 1890–1914* (Austin: University of Texas Press, 1970). For details on immigrants in Argentina, see Eugene F. Sofer, "Immigration and Entrepreneurship in Buenos Aires, 1890–1927: The Jewish Case" (paper presented at Pacific Coast Council on Latin American Studies, Tempe, Ariz., 1976).

47.    Quoted in Samuel L. Baily, *Labor, Nationalism and Politics in Argentina* (New Brunswick, N.J.: Rutgers University Press, 1967), p. 25.

48.    David Rock, *Politics in Argentina, 1890–1930: The Rise and Fall of Radicalism* (Cambridge, Eng.: Cambridge University Press, 1975), is an excellent analysis of the evolution of the Radical Party's role within the Argentine political system.

49.    For details of research underway on this right-wing group, see Sandra F. McGee, "The Liga Patriótica Argentina and the Defense of Order," *Latinamericanist*, 13, no. 2 (March 1978) (Gainesville: Center for Latin American Studies, University of Florida).

50.    The Argentine Socialist Party has been given a systematic analysis in Richard J. Walter, *The Socialist Party of Argentina, 1890–1930* (Austin: Institute of Latin American Studies, University of Texas, 1977).

51.    My analysis of labor movements in Brazil relies heavily on Boris Fausto, *Trabalho urbano e conflicto social, 1890–1920* (São Paulo: DIFEL, 1976); Sheldon L. Maram, "Anarcho-syndicalism in Brazil," in *Proceedings of the Pacific Coast Council on Latin American Studies*, 4 (1975): 101–116; Maram, "Labor and the Left in Brazil, 1890–1921: A Movement Aborted," *Hispanic American Historical Review*, 57, no. 2 (May 1977): 254–272. Both of the foregoing are largely drawn from Maram's "Anarchism, Immigrants, and the Brazilian Labor Movement, 1890–1920" (Ph.D dissertation, University of California, Santa Barbara, 1972). The latter work was a major source for Fausto. An earlier work which gives a wealth of information is Azis Simão, *Sindicato e estado: Suas relações na formação do proletariado de São Paulo* (São Paulo: DIFEL, 1966), which should be supplemented by Paula Beiguelman, *Os companheiros de São Paulo* (São Paulo: Edições Símbolo, 1977). Important for the decade of the 1920s is Paulo Sérgio Pinheiro, *Política e trabalho no Brasil* (Rio de Janeiro: Paz e Terra, 1975). Considerable detail is offered in John W. F. Dulles, *Anarchists and Communists in Brazil, 1900–1935* (Austin: University of Texas Press, 1973). Excellent bibliographical surveys may be found in Leôncio Martins Rodrigues and Fábio Antônio Munhoz, "Bibliografia sobre trabalhadores e sindicatos no Brasil," *Estudos CEBRAP*, no. 7 (January–March 1974): 153–171, and Luiz Werneck Vianna, "Estudos sobre sindicalismo e movimento operário: Resenha de algumas tendências," *Boletim Informativo e Bibliográfico de Ciências Sociais* (Rio de Janeiro), no. 3 (1978): 1–40 (supplement to *Dados*, no. 17 [1978]).

52.    Sheldon L. Maram, "The Immigrant and the Brazilian Labor Move-

ment, 1890–1920," in *Essays Concerning the Socioeconomic History of Brazil and Portuguese India,* ed. Dauril Aldon and Warren Dean (Gainesville: University Presses of Florida, 1977), 178–210.

53. Sheldon L. Maram, "Urban Labor and Social Change in the 1920's," forthcoming in the *Luso-Brazilian Review.* Maram argues that after 1920 the Anarchist tactics (general strikes, especially) played into the hands of the government, while at the same time alienating union members, who wanted better pay and working conditions, not political confrontations.

54. There is a summary of the laws in Alberto da Rocha Barros, *Origens e evolução da legislação trabalhista* (Rio de Janeiro: Laemmert, 1969), pp. 49–50. An excellent historical account of the creation of the social security programs in Brazil is given in James M. Malloy, "Social Security Policy and the Working Class in Twentieth-Century Brazil," *Journal of Inter-American Studies and World Affairs,* 19, no. 1 (February 1977): 35–59, taken from his forthcoming study of the origins and consequences of Brazil's social security system, which Professor Malloy kindly permitted me to read in manuscript.

55. This point is emphasized in Michael L. Conniff, "The Tenentes in Power: A New Perspective on the Brazilian Revolution of 1930," *Journal of Latin American Studies,* 10, Part 1 (May 1976): 61–82.

56. For a well-documented study of the Communist Party, see Ronald H. Chilcote, *The Brazilian Communist Party: Conflict and Integration, 1922–1972* (New York: Oxford University Press, 1974).

57. This analysis of Chile is largely drawn from Peter DeShazo, "Urban Workers and Labor Unions in Chile, 1902–1927" (Ph.D. dissertation, University of Wisconsin, Madison, 1977), which presents a wealth of information on living conditions and union organization, showing clearly the effectiveness of the Anarchist leadership.

58. The standard account of the struggle leading to the adoption of the Chilean labor code is James O. Morris, *Elites, Intellectuals, and Consensus: A Study of the Social Question and the Industrial Relations System in Chile* (Ithaca: New York State School of Industrial and Labor Relations, Cornell University, 1966), which includes a very careful exposition of the differing grounds on which elite spokesmen proposed to justify and codify a state-sponsored system of labor relations and social welfare.

59. The political background to the intervention of the military in 1924 is given in Frederick M. Nunn, *Chilean Politics, 1920–1931: The Honorable Mission of the Armed Forces* (Albuquerque: University of New Mexico Press, 1970).

60. For an excellent study of this party and its origins, see Paul W. Drake, *Socialism and Populism in Chile, 1932–52* (Urbana: University of Illinois Press, 1978).

61. The relationship between labor unions and left-wing political parties

in Chile is well treated in Angell, *Politics and the Labour Movement in Chile;* Frederick B. Pike, in his *Chile and the United States, 1880–1962* (Notre Dame: Notre Dame University Press, 1963), described 1920–1933 as the period in which "Chile Almost Breaks with the Past."

62. A recent overview of the 1930s in Argentina is presented in Mark Falcoff and Ronald H. Dolkart, "Political Developments," in *Prologue to Perón: Argentina in Depression and War, 1930–1943*, ed. Falcoff and Dolkart (Berkeley: University of California Press, 1975), pp. 31–56. The most convincing account of the origins and significance of the coup of 1930 is Peter H. Smith, "The Breakdown of Democracy in Argentina, 1916–30," in *The Breakdown of Democratic Regimes: Latin America*, ed. Juan Linz and Alfred Stepan (Baltimore: Johns Hopkins University Press, 1978), pp. 3–27.

63. The most balanced systematic evaluation of the Perón era up to 1955 is Peter Waldmann, *Der Peronismus, 1943–1955* (Hamburg: Hoffmann und Campe, 1974). Perón's death in 1974 may finally make possible a scholarly biography of this important figure.

64. We lack a thorough investigation into the GOU. The question of officer opinion toward labor is discussed in Robert A. Potash, *The Army and Politics in Argentina, 1928–1945: Yrigoyen to Perón* (Stanford: Stanford University Press, 1969), pp. 227–229, 259–261. As Waldman notes, the exact historical role of the GOU in the 1943 coup and the subsequent government policies has yet to be clearly established (*Der Peronismus*, pp. 156–162).

65. For an analysis of the circumstances that led General Lanusse to decide in favor of Perón's return, see David Rock, "The Survival and Destruction of Peronism," in *Argentina in the Twentieth Century*, ed. Rock (Pittsburgh: University of Pittsburgh Press, 1975), pp. 179–221. For an interpretation sympathetic to the armed revolutionary line in Argentina, see François Gèze and Alain Labrousse, *Argentine: Révolution et contre-révolutions* (Paris: Editions du Seuil, 1975).

66. Thomas E. Skidmore, "Failure in Brazil: From Popular Front to Armed Revolt," *Journal of Contemporary History*, 5, no. 3: 137–157.

67. A perceptive analysis of Brazilian labor legislation and the ideological background of its adoption may be found in Luiz Werneck Vianna, *Liberalismo e sindicato no Brasil* (Rio de Janeiro: Paz e Terra, 1976). The growth of the labor relations and social welfare systems and the manner in which they have been modified by the authoritarian governments since 1964 is given in Maria Hermínia Tavares de Almeida, "O sindicato no Brasil: Novos problems, velhas estruturas," *Debate & Crítica*, no. 6 (July 1975): 49–74. A careful analysis of the Brazilian labor relations system, with emphasis on the populist mobilization of the early 1960s, is given in Kenneth Paul Erickson, *The Brazilian Corporative State and Working-Class Politics* (Berkeley: University of California Press, 1977).

68. The relative importance of the workers' spontaneous mobilization in 1953 has been lucidly analyzed in José Alvaro Moisés, *Greve de massa e crise política: Estudo da greve dos 300 mil em São Paulo—1953/54* (São Paulo: Ed. Polis, 1978). Moisés is especially critical of the Communist Party's decision to channel the workers' commissions back into the official union structure.

69. The study of Brazilian political party history has been inhibited by the widely held view that Brazilian parties since 1945 have been little more than agglomerations of personalistic associations. In fact, electoral data for the 1945–1964 period do not support that interpretation; the data deserve much more careful study than has yet been the case, a point argued effectively in Maria do Carmo C. Campello de Souza, *Estado e partidos políticos no Brasil (1930–1964)* (São Paulo: Ed. Alfa-Omega, 1976).

70. Hobart Spalding posits three variables as having influenced the development of Latin American urban labor movements: (1) "fluctuations of the international economy and decisions taken by governments in advanced capitalist nations"; (2) "the composition of, and tensions between, the international and the local ruling classes"; and (3) "the composition, structure, and historical formation of the working class" (Spalding, *Organized Labor in Latin America*, p. ix).

71. Howard J. Wiarda, "Corporative Origins of the Iberian and Latin American Labor Relations Systems," *Studies in Comparative International Development*, 13, no. 1 (Spring 1978): 3–37.

72. Ruth Berins Collier and David Collier, "Inducements versus Constraints: Disaggregating 'Corporatism,'" *American Political Science Review*, forthcoming. Ruth Collier is presently engaged in a comparative study of the incorporation of the "popular sector" and regime evolution in Brazil and Mexico, which includes analysis of policies toward labor, both in law and in practice.

73. An excellent start toward this analysis has been made in James Paul McConarty, "The Defense of the Working Class in the Brazilian Chamber of Deputies, 1917–1920," (M.A. thesis, Tulane University, 1973).

74. This is the point pursued in Cain, "The Challenge of Segmented Labor Market Theories." Examples of "dual labor market" analyses are given in Kannappan, *Studies of Urban Labour Market Behavior*, which includes a study of wage differentials in São Paulo's manufacturing firms by José Pastore, Archibald Haller, and Hernando Gomez Buendia.

75. On these questions there is a rapidly growing literature, of which the following is a brief sampling: Douglas H. Graham, "Interstate Migration and the Industrial Labor Force in Center-South Brazil," *The Journal of Developing Areas*, 12, no. 1 (October 1977): 31–46; Bruce H. Herrick, *Urban Migration and Economic Development in Chile* (Cambridge, Mass.: MIT Press, 1965); Vicente Vázquez-Presedo, *El*

*caso argentino: Migración de factores, comercio exterior y desarrollo, 1875–1914* (Buenos Aires: EUDEBA, 1971); Donald B. Keesing, "Employment and Lack of Employment in Mexico, 1900–70," in *Quantitative Latin American Studies: Methods and Findings*, ed. James W. Wilkie and Kenneth Ruddle, Statistical Abstract of Latin America, Supplement 6 (Los Angeles: UCLA Latin American Center, 1977), pp. 3–21; Thomas H. Holloway, "Creating the Reserve Army? The Immigration Program of São Paulo, 1886–1930," *International Review*, 12 (1978): 187–209.

76. Julio Samuel Valenzuela, "The Chilean Labor Movement: The Institutionalization of Conflict," in *Chile: Politics and Society*, ed. Arturo Valenzuela and J. Samuel Valenzuela (New Brunswick, N.J.: Transaction Books, 1976), p. 156.

77. Angell, *Politics and the Labour Movement in Chile*, pp. 177, 192–193.

78. Ibid., p. 101.

79. The militancy of the more politically ambitious elements within the official labor movement is well analyzed in Erickson, *The Brazilian Corporative State.*

80. A seminal analysis of this process is Barrington Moore, Jr., *Social Origins of Dictatorship and Democracy* (Boston: Beacon Press, 1966). For a meticulous examination of the relationship between economic development and political systems in Latin America, see David Collier, "Timing of Economic Growth and Regime Characterization in Latin America," *Comparative Politics*, 7 (April 1975): 331–359.

# University of St. Thomas B. K. Smith Lectures in History

1958. Carlton J. H. Hayes, "Some Uses and Abuses of History."
1959. Kurt Von Schuschnigg, *Central Europe: Past Adventure, Present Labor, Future Vision.*
1961. John U. Nef, *Religion and the Study of Man.*
1962. E. E. Y. Hales, *The First Vatican Council.*
1963. Wallace K. Ferguson, *Erasmus and Christian Humanism.*
1964. Oscar Halecki, *Poland and Christendom.*
1965. Robert F. Byrnes, *Russia a Century Ago.*
1966. Richard E. Sullivan, *The Medieval Church: A View from the 1960s.*
1967. Raymond H. Schmandt, *The Crusades: Origin of an Ecumenical Problem.*
1968. Francis Oakley, *Kingship and the Gods: The Western Apostasy.*
1970. Josep L. Altholz, *The Conscience of Lord Acton.*
1971. David Herlihy, *Women in Medieval Society.*
1972. Lewis Hanke, *Spanish Viceroys in America.*
1974. Ernest May and Walter LaFeber, *The Impact of War on the United States in the Twentieth Century.*
1976. J. R. Pole and Gordon Wood, *Social Radicalism and the Idea of Equality in the American Revolution.*
1978. E. Bradford Burns and Thomas E. Skidmore, "Popular Challenges and Elite Responses in Latin America, 1850–1930."

(Lectures from 1959 through 1976 have been published by the University of St. Thomas. For information, write the History Department, University of St. Thomas, 3812 Montrose Boulevard, Houston, Texas 77006.)